HOW I NAVIGATED THE W

MULTIFAMILY REA

TO CLOSE MY FIRST DEAL, AND HOW YOU CAN TOO!

FOR SUCH A TIME AS THIS

RANDY MILLET

For Such a Time as This:
How I Navigated the World of Multifamily Real Estate to Close
My First Deal, and How You Can Too!
© 2024 by Randy Millet
All rights reserved.

ISBN: 979-8-9915272-0-0

Norstac Publishing
74 Patterson Dr.
Chalmette, LA 70043

This book is a work of non-fiction. Verbal permission has been granted by all named individuals I interacted with in the story. All other sources are credited in the reference section.

Edited and illustrated by Collin Millet

Published in the United States of America
First Edition, 2024
Printed in the United States of America

FOR SUCH A TIME AS THIS

HOW I NAVIGATED THE WORLD OF MULTIFAMILY REAL ESTATE TO CLOSE MY FIRST DEAL, AND HOW YOU CAN TOO!

RANDY MILLET

TO LISA, LILA, AND SAMUEL

ACKNOWLEDGEMENTS

To my wife, Lisa:

You have supported me since day one. You recognized my passion to push beyond my boundaries and have enabled me to begin fulfilling my call. I couldn't ask for a better mother to my children, or a better partner to journey through life with. In addition to all of your support, you have always believed in me. Thank you for being my biggest fan.

To my parents:

You taught me to dream. You raised me by example and believed in everything I've ever attempted. The man I've become is because of you.

To my brother:

When I sent you the first few pages, I never expected us to find a new layer of our relationship. Working with you on this project has been one of the best things we've done together. Your talent for editing and ability to help me articulate my story has surprised me and exceeded my expectations. I look forward to our next endeavor.

To Daniel and Sam:

I cannot sufficiently express how grateful I am for your mentorship and friendship. All of the guidance and wisdom that you've poured into your students is worth much more than you've ever earned. May God continue to bless and use you to your fullest potential as you continue to be an inspiration to us all.

To Chris and my AREA family:

As the adage says, we can go further together, and this book is not a story of MY success but OUR success. When one of us wins, we all win. I can't wait to see what the future holds for all of us, and know that I cherish our relationships and our community.

EDITOR'S NOTE

I have a special connection to both the story and author of this book. Randy is my brother, and I have had the incredible pleasure of riding shotgun for this entire experience. Randy has always aspired to be successful. While success in real estate investing is a good indicator of that, he has always been successful to me. I've seen the life he's led and the man he has become. I was there for many of life's greatest accomplishments, and I've seen his many achievements come to pass. When he began this journey as a real estate investor, I believed in him. Now, at an age where many settle in and make plans for retirement, Randy has resisted such fate. He has started a brand new career in a very daunting and competitive field. Many never dare to attempt such a risky endeavor, but Randy has never feared the challenge.

While you have the advantage of reading the story in full, I stood by and watched when there was no end in sight. With each excitement and disappointment, I watched as Randy navigated uncharted waters on his own. I witnessed him conquer each trial and stayed unmoved. I spoke to him only hours after one of the greatest setbacks of his career and he said, "I have peace." I was impressed when he succeeded, but seeing his unwavering resolve during the struggle was what impacted me most. After reading just a few chapters, I told him, "If the rest of this book is anything like these chapters, then you have to write this book." Somehow, the chapters to come were an even greater triumph.

I strongly believe in this story and the impact it may have on you. This is a tale of the underdog as he walks the hero's journey. It will inspire anyone looking for a spark. This book has given me the drive to build a better future for my family. My path will not be real estate investing, but this book has opened my mind to the possibilities in my life. God has a call for each of us, and the call is greater than us. While reading, I hope you get the chance to realize the path God has called you to walk. I highly recommend you read this book and share it with others. This is inspiration to empower you to become the person you are meant to be.

_____

COLLIN MILLET

TABLE OF CONTENTS

TABLE OF CONTENTS CONTINUED

FOREWORD

There are certain moments in life you just don't forget. For others it may be something they saw, a story they heard, or perhaps something they felt. For me, I've always had a fascination towards quotes. As an entrepreneur that's always looking for ways to solve problems faster, cheaper and/or even easier, I appreciate the very nature of what quotes are. Which really if you think about it, are a way of condensing years of wisdom, pain, and learning, into one or two simple sentences.

Many say if you don't know how to articulate the most complex concepts of your craft, into a simple paragraph that even a 5th grader can understand, you don't truly understand it to begin with, or you don't have any interest in catering to children, which is also a valid point!

The first time I heard this quote, I knew my life changed at that moment. It was, as I mentioned earlier, a certain moment in my life I just didn't forget. Many times these quotes come to me from scripture or from my time with God, but this particular quote is used and said by the Navy Seals.

"As seals, we don't rise to the level of the occasion, we sink to the level of our training, and that's why we train so hard."

As someone who's had the honor of being able to coach the author of this book, along with the hundreds around the country, I've had my fair share of clients who've said,

"Coach, I'm nervous."

To which my response 99% of the time would be:

"Well... should you be?"

I think this response can apply to almost everything in life, even beyond just investing in rental properties. The reality of the world we live in today, is that for 90% of people who want better, but aren't willing to BE BETTER, think better, or even eat better, they absolutely one thousand percent SHOULD be nervous. In fact, for the 90%, nervousness, as opposed to confidence, is the correct and appropriate response.

We have a record amount of people in our country that struggle with obesity and health. But considering the choices the average person makes when it comes to diet, nutrition and exercise, can we really say we're surprised? And with the gradual rise in social media usage and the decline of community, are we surprised with the state of mental health in this country as well? I'd be willing to bet most people nowadays don't even know the names of their neighbors.

I have a friend thats very well known in the real estate investing industry who once said to me in passing:

"I think people should do whatever they can to get to a point where success is NOT a surprise"

And in the case of the author of this book, Randy Millet, that is absolutely the case. I, as his coach, am not one bit surprised that he's successful as a real estate investor & entrepreneur. Considering that he has,

- Attended almost every weekly training we host for our community of students.

- Invested into showing up to our live events.

- Have sacrificed time to book 1 on 1 sessions with not just myself but our support coaches.

- Has completed every task we advised him to do within the method.

Randy has done exactly what every other successful client before him has done, which is show up, follow the process, take action, and don't give up. But considering you're reading this book, you'll just see for yourself how it all unfolded!

I hope you all enjoy reading it, as much as I've enjoyed being part of it.

DANIEL KWAK

PREFACE

My name is Randy Millet, and I'm a husband and father of two. I lead worship at my church on Sundays and I'm a Technical Sergeant in the Louisiana Air National Guard. At the time of writing this book, I am really just getting started as a real estate investor. I began to write this book as my deal was in progress much like a journal, but I wasn't sure exactly what the book was even going to be. As you'll read, the struggles and obstacles I had to navigate were happening and being documented in real time. The lessons I learned, mistakes I made, and obstacles I overcame are all on display. You'll see how I used every tool at my disposal to transform myself in the world of business. There are several nuggets of knowledge I've gleaned from my mentors and other books that I have included. My hope is that you are entertained by my story, inspired by the lessons provided, and propelled to take the action necessary to achieve your potential in whichever field you chose.

COMFORT IS A DRUG.
IT'S ADDICTIVE. GIVE
A MAN REGULAR SEX,
GOOD FOOD, AND CHEAP
ENTERTAINMENT, AND
HE'LL THROW HIS
AMBITIONS RIGHT OUT
OF THE WINDOW. THE
COMFORT ZONE IS WHERE
DREAMS GO TO DIE.

———————————

HENRY CAVILL

CHAPTER ONE

LIGHTING THE FIRE

. ────────────────

It's Tuesday, July 23, 2024. I am under contract for an apartment building totaling 10 units in New Orleans, LA. I just sent a series of emails to a representative from the title company, my insurance broker, and my mortgage brokers. I've already transferred funds from my limited partner (LP) to my business account, which will be used for the down payment. For this deal, my LP will not hold any equity. My LP will receive interest-only payments until the original investment is paid back. I don't have a background in real estate, business, or finance, and I didn't come from money. My parents are pastors of a small church outside New Orleans, and my wife is a clinical pharmacist. I have a three-year-old daughter, and a newborn son. I don't have a college education. I have spent most of my career full-time in the Louisiana Air National Guard after enlisting at the age of 18. I am an everyday working-class man. I am not special. ***This is my first deal.***

When I least expected it, something as simple as a YouTube video lit a spark that would change the course of my life and set me on a path I never thought I would end up on. It didn't seem life-altering at the time, but it would illuminate the world around me. Until that day, I had been content with my life's trajectory; but unexpectedly, a seed was planted—a seed that would grow discontent in allowing my life to be dictated by someone else. Once this epiphany took root, it became impossible to ignore. It formed a thirst for knowledge, and that knowledge forced me to take action. A transformation took place, and once my eyes were opened, they would never be shut again.

As a child, I was raised in a Christian household and taught the value of hard work, loyalty, love of country, and the importance of a relationship with God. I was taught that God has a plan for me, and if I submitted to His will, He would use me to my full potential. God's timing, however, is not our timing, and there were many things I had yet to learn.

Right after high school, I enlisted in the Louisiana Air National Guard and have been in active duty status since 2014. My official title is Aircraft Armament Systems Technician, which is just fancy for loading weapons on our F-15 fighter jets and performing maintenance on the weapons systems. In June of 2022, I was sent on temporary deployment to Langley Air Force Base in Hampton, Virginia, to provide air support for the President anytime he left the White House. A typical day started at 7:00 A.M. with a few missile movements and jet launching and recovering until 3:00 P.M. Then, I'd change clothes and play 18 holes at the golf course on base. The lofty goal I set for myself was to get my golf score into the 80s before I returned home. I know what you're thinking: your tax dollars were hard at work, but it was my outlet to relieve work stress and cope with being separated from my family.

Back home in New Orleans, my wife, Lisa, was working full time as a pharmacist and caring for our daughter, Lila, who was 18 months old. For me, my daily routine was a sort of Groundhog Day. It was predictable enough to keep my stress level low and exciting enough to keep me complacent and comfortable. There is nothing more dangerous than being comfortable.

I never dreamt of being rich. I may have had daydreams about winning the lottery, but I've never had the burning desire to reach outside my boundaries in search of something more. I often thought of myself as someone with the intelligence of an entrepreneur, but this was nothing more than fleeting anecdotes used in conversation. I was part of the "If I wanted to" crowd. It would always start with something like "If I really wanted to start my own business..." and end with, "but I don't have the time."

I'm sure you've met people like this—the jack-of-all-trades type who are still the master of none. They have enough talking points to be a guest on Fox Business but lack the ability and drive to put one foot in front of the other. They're the first to tell you how "risky" what you're doing is and all the ways it will go wrong, as if they have more financial insight than Jim Cramer, Warren Buffett, and the chairman of the Fed. Maybe they've read books such as *Rich Dad Poor Dad* or watched some YouTube shorts of Jordan Belfort saying, "Sell me this pen," but when it comes to personal finance, they live paycheck to paycheck. They are drowning in credit card debt but are obsessed over their credit score. They curse big banks as they watch their 401(k) dwindle.

People like this are a dime a dozen because they live in the pursuit of sitting on the couch after work. They strive for the weekend and nothing more. They work for someone else because they trust their future is in better hands with an employer than with themselves. There's a good chance that you are one of those people. I was, too, until I took action once and for all. In June of 2022, I had a brush with destiny, and something fundamentally changed in me. I didn't know it then, but that burning desire to push beyond my limits, reject comfort, and strive to expand my borders had been lit. It caused me to question things I had heard my entire life.

While at work waiting for jets to land, I was lying on the floor comfortably resting my head on my backpack as I mindlessly scrolled through YouTube videos. I wasn't looking for anything in particular; I was just passing time. As I scrolled, a thumbnail caught my eye. It was a video titled "Pay Off Your House in 5-7 Years." In this 17-minute video, Sam Kwak laid out a financial strategy that I'd never seen before as he explained how using a home equity line of credit (HELOC) in conjunction with velocity banking would allow me to pay off my mortgage and get out of debt. If this was true, it could be life-changing. Who wouldn't want to shed the burden of a 30-year mortgage? Of course, this could be a scam since social media is littered with charlatans selling modern-day snake oil, but this definitely warranted some research.

Sam and Daniel Kwak are brothers who immigrated to Chicago from South Korea as children. I learned that their dad is a pastor, which was immediately endearing because so was mine. They possess the drive that allows them to seize opportunity and create tremendous success. They currently own eight businesses and have helped entrepreneurs get started in real estate investing. You can read their inspiring story in Daniel Kwak's book, *0 to 75 Units in 1 Year*, but for now, Sam was just another person on YouTube offering something that seemed too good to be true: financial freedom!

While I was skeptical, something about the way the information was presented gained my trust. The math, well… mathed. The strategy was solid, and the company had good reviews, so I thought it was at least worth booking a call. After all, the discovery call was free so I figured since I had nothing but time on my hands, there was nothing to lose. Once I booked the call, I tried to regurgitate my 17-minute YouTube education to my wife to keep her in the loop, but I may as well have been speaking a foreign language. Einstein said, "If you can't explain it simply, you don't understand it well enough." I definitely didn't understand it fully, but for the first time I caught the vision. After discussing it together, I booked the call.

Hello Randy,

It appears that you're interested in the Accelerated Banking Consulting program, but you want more details and information on what's included. I've created a page that breaks everything down. Here's the link to see the full details: ###

Regards,
Accelerated Banking Consulting Program

During my discovery call, all of my questions were answered, and I gained a better understanding of the strategy. I was guided through my financial information to project how long it would take to pay off my house. For a one-time fee, I could become a client of the coaching program, which would ensure I was set up, ready to go, and on track to paying off my house. I was sold. I signed up to be a client and paid the entire fee in full, right there on the spot. I felt a stirring that couldn't be ignored; it meant it was time to take action.

My father often said,

"No one can make Randy do anything, but if he sets his mind to it, nobody can stop him."

I've always shown a level of determination. At the age of

12, I taught myself to play the drums, and when I was 20, I taught myself piano. I wasn't professionally trained; I just decided one day that I wanted to play music, so I did. Since then, I've learned multiple instruments, and I sing and write songs too. One day, on a whim, I decided to build a wooden ice chest holder out of fence boards. That was easy enough, so next I made an end table which led to an epoxy table, and when my wife was expecting our first child I built a beautiful mahogany dresser for our daughter. I did the same with food. After a lifetime of barely being able to make a ham sandwich, one day I decided to teach myself the art of cooking. Before long, I was making dishes à la Julia Child and Thomas Keller. Whether it's food, music, or woodworking, I've always had an urge to create. I often explore new outlets for my creativity, and they soon become a passion. Once I'm passionate about something, I have a determination that simply won't allow me to quit.

After watching Sam's video, I recognized that spark that would become a relentless pursuit. Once I set my mind to it, my mind would not let go. This time, instead of writing a song or building a piece of furniture, I would be creating a new financial outcome for my family and myself. Ideally, I would have my wife sitting next to me on the call, but we were 1,000 miles apart, so I flew solo on this one. Lisa and I operate on trust and always consult each other before making big decisions; however, given the unusual circumstances, I pulled the trigger. I knew she wouldn't be happy, and I was right. While what I'd done was not advisable, a fire had been lit inside me. I knew in my gut that this was an opportunity we needed to jump on. After discussing things, she reluctantly trusted that I made the right decision for our family. Now that we were on the same page, I had to follow through. I took on the responsibility, and I had to deliver. I was determined to see this through.

Full of motivation, I quickly sprang into action. I started working my way through the checklist and began interviewing banks to set up the HELOC. The program gave me a list of questions to ask each bank to assist me when vetting them. While I'm usually outgoing and confident in person, I was timid and insecure on the phone with bankers, so making these phone calls was an uncomfortable experience. This was their world, not mine, but as I stumbled through each call, I got my first taste of the world of business. They were using terms like DTI (debt-to-income), LTV (loan-to-value), and six-month treasury. I did my best to sound professional, but I was wet behind the ears.

I have a pretty good memory and can usually keep

track of things without taking notes or using a filing system, but I've never conducted a business transaction of this size before. It soon became clear that my old habits must die and things would have to change. As with any new endeavor, I would have to develop new skills. The amount of information I needed to process a HELOC became overwhelming, especially when interviewing multiple banks. It became a headache, so I had to stay focused and get organized.

After disqualifying myself with a few different banks, I started to lose steam. That fire of motivation was barely a flicker at this point. My credit and LTV were major issues, and I didn't like issues. I expected a smooth and easy transaction, and I wasn't prepared to fight through obstacles. I fizzled out. Honestly, I would rather play golf and mindlessly scroll through social media than continue my financial education. Deep down, I knew this wasn't the right move, but the fire was out. My motivation ceased, and I gave up. Just like my dad said, "No one can make Randy do anything," and that was true, now more than ever.

When motivation dwindles, discipline must take over. Motivation is the tinder of a fire that lights quickly and burns bright, but it doesn't last long. To keep the fire burning, it needs big logs at the bottom that burn slowly to continually fuel the fire. Discipline is the fuel, and I suddenly realized I was out of it. I expected my motivation to carry me through the entire process, but just as a strong wind will extinguish tinder, a few obstacles caused me to give up. Obstacles are inevitable. In fact, they are necessary because without obstacles, discipline would never develop. Obstacles weed out the weak, but to the disciplined, every obstacle narrows one's focus. The same wind that will extinguish tinder will feed the flame. It provides oxygen to the fire and causes the fuel to burn. What separates me now from when I began is realizing that every obstacle is another opportunity. Unfortunately, at this point, I didn't have the discipline to endure the obstacles, and I allowed the fire to be extinguished.

After my deployment, I returned home and resumed my normal activities. It was my regularly scheduled mind-numbing mediocrity. The alarm would sound at 4:30 A.M., and *Groundhog Day* would ensue. Once we got off work, Lisa and I wrestled the baby to bed, and with the remaining hours of the evening, I would usually fall asleep watching some useless show that held no bearing on my future. The repetition of comfort had nearly taken root once more until the day I was dreading finally came. Lisa asked,

"What ever happened with the HELOC? We paid a lot of money for that program. Why didn't we ever close?"

These were all valid questions without valid answers. The real answer was that I had given up because I didn't have the mental fortitude to follow through. I wasn't who I thought I was. The fire inside me never stood a chance because I didn't have the fuel to stay lit.

"Maybe you should give that guy a call."

Thank God she brought it up. I made promises and was letting her down and letting myself down. I promised that I could improve our financial situation, and now it was time to follow through. I'm not normally a person who gives up so easily, but this was a different beast. I'm used to challenges, but they are always within my control. If my coq au vin is undercooked, it's because I took it out of the oven prematurely. If my table isn't level, it's because I didn't measure twice and cut once. But in these uncharted waters, it seemed these obstacles were out of my control. I dove into the water headfirst without knowing how deep it would be.

At my wife's request, I booked another call with my coach, and we discussed my previous obstacles and got back to work. The obstacles didn't magically go away, but I refocused, and in February of 2023, I closed on my HELOC. I've had lots of important moments in my life: graduating from basic military training, getting married, and having my daughter, to name a few. Without diminishing the aforementioned, closing on my HELOC would prove to be one of the most important moments of my life.

I hadn't realized it yet, but this one action set things in motion that would bring me to the very place I am now. That HELOC was the first log on the fire. It was the catalyst. I finally broke free from the norm. I had taken a step toward financial freedom. I moved from one category to another. I was no longer participating in the scripted financial narrative: work, pay taxes, retire, and die. I was no longer going to be stuck in a 30-year mortgage that financial institutions display as the only option. I felt like I was beating the system. The fire of desire, reduced to smoldering coals, was ablaze once again. If not for that moment, that victory, and that mindset alteration, who would I be today? It was just one step in a different direction, but it changed the course of my life forever.

FOR OF HIM, AND
THROUGH HIM, AND
TO HIM, ARE ALL THINGS:
TO WHOM BE GLORY
FOR EVER. AMEN.

———————————

ROMANS 11:36 KJV

CHAPTER TWO

TO GOD BE THE GLORY

— · ————————————

Lisa and I got married in March 2018. We were renting from her parents when we first got married, but soon after, we purchased a home. It was a two-bedroom, one-bath house with a garage, which I turned into my woodworking shop. The house was built by her grandfather in the 1940s and has been in her family ever since. While we loved it, we needed more space once she was pregnant with my daughter, so we bought a bigger house and started renting out the smaller property. I had never rented a house before, but luckily, we found great tenants who are still renting it today. We were earning a whopping $200 a month from rent. While that's hardly enough cash flow to be excited about, I knew we were gaining equity. I figured we'd eventually sell it and enjoy a nice payday. It was the smart thing to do, and I thought we were doing well. We were comfortable.

It wasn't until my HELOC experience that I really started to see things differently. I had seen behind a curtain that I was never supposed to know existed. I quickly became disenchanted with the idea of staying in the military until I was 60. I woke up early and worked out in the elements because my job required intensive manual labor. It's not without its benefits. I got to travel often, and I had free health insurance, tax advantages, military discounts, and security. It's an honorable profession, and lots of people excel throughout their military careers, as did I. That was my life's trajectory. I was thankful for the life I had, but suddenly, I wanted more. I felt a stirring in my gut like never before. I knew that God had His hand on me and that I was on the cusp of a calling.

I started reading books that furthered my financial education. I learned about different strategies not commonly used by the general public. I had always shied away from credit cards and was taught that debt is bad, but with my new outlook, I found value in credit cards and how best to leverage points to save money. I began to research articles about stock prices and read the latest reports on mortgage rates that I had previously ignored. I was now aware of my financial ignorance, and this was the first step. I was discovering that there was a better way, and I could no longer stand by and watch from the sidelines. I had to explore this new way of thinking further.

I no longer thought ignorance was bliss but now realized it was a hindrance. It's a straitjacket to insight; a locked chamber to success. A society does not progress by being content in its own ignorance. It's the quest for knowledge that drives humanity forward. Likewise, the quest for knowledge will drive your personal progress. In business, they say "grow or die," and the same can be said for your life. In order to grow, you need to have knowledge of knowledge. You need to know what you don't know and then strive to learn it. It's the knowledge itself that empowers the pursuit.

It wasn't until a few weeks after I closed on my HELOC with help from the Accelerated Banking Educational Program (ABC) that I began to really learn about who the Kwak brothers are. Sam does most of the education for ABC, but I came across another video, and this time, Daniel Kwak was explaining the fundamentals of real estate investing. I listened as he shared how they began purchasing apartment buildings in their early 20s with seller financing. A huge revelatory moment was how they leveraged other people's money to fund their deals. As I watched video after video, I felt the fire again. It was that same fire in my belly as when I was lying on the floor passing time in Virginia. "I can do this." I wasn't the same person as before. I had pushed through my dwindling motivation into discipline. I broke from social norms and took a chance. I was no longer asleep at the wheel; now, I was awake, in control, and ready.

I couldn't get through the videos fast enough. I was chomping at the bit. I ordered Daniel's book online before I finished the last video, the one where he gives a link to get a free copy of his book. I didn't even care. That was the best $14 I had ever spent. Until recently, I had honestly never been much of a reader. While I liked the idea of reading books, I rarely engaged. I would buy books and rarely finish them, but when this book arrived, I devoured it. With each page, I gained more knowledge about how to enter this world that seemed closed off to the rest of us. It was in his book that I learned about his background and that we shared the same faith. I could tell that he was driven but not braggadocious. When I finished reading his book, I prayed and thanked God for opening this door. I knew that His hand was in this and that this was the next step. I knew this more than I had known anything in my life.

Years prior, one Sunday morning at church, I received a word from God. He told me that I was going to help finance His kingdom. He told me that I would receive riches, not for riches' sake, but for the sake of the ministry. I believed that would happen, but I never knew when or how. The truth is, God had a lot of work to do in me first. My past is illuminated with miracles of God's supernatural provision. In the years after Hurricane Katrina, God sent countless people to my community who donated time, resources, and money to further the work of His kingdom. On that Sunday morning, God told me one day I would be that person. I would be in the financial position to bless where He tells me to bless and sow where He tells me to sow. And it would all be for His glory. I received that word and continuously told God that I would fulfill my call and do His will.

My path was becoming clear; I knew that God had anointed me for this, but at this point, I had no idea how much work would have to be done first. Daniel's book made it seem so simple, and truth be told, it is simple. Anyone with a grade school-level math education can learn how to calculate CAP rates and underwrite a deal. Anyone can make phone calls and send emails. It really is simple, but simple does not mean easy.

Watching videos and reading books was only going to take me so far. I needed proper training, mentorship, and guidance if I stood any chance at learning this industry. While reading his book, I learned of their coaching program for real estate investors. I wasted no time in booking the call, and I ran it by Lisa first this time. Since the cost was bound to be significantly more than ABC, I made sure to schedule a time when my wife could sit next to me on the call, and this is when I met Chris Morrow.

Chris had been working for Daniel in his real estate coaching program called First Deal Mentor for about three years (later changed to Accelerated Real Estate Academy, which I will refer to as AREA moving forward). Chris is one of the most genuine people I know, and I'm lucky to consider him a friend. He grew up in the Midwest and has a background in sales. We come from different worlds, but even from our first conversation, I could tell our perspectives were similar. A bond started to form. This wasn't a typical sales call. There weren't any "act now" lines or used car salesman jargon. He was sincere, easy to talk to, and to the point. He would come to serve as a valuable source of inspiration.

I told him why I wanted to get started in real estate and explained my financial goals. I remember when he told me that if I wanted to supplement Lisa's and my income, I'd have to get 50 doors and raise $2 million in capital. Those numbers were enormous to me. Then he told us how much the coaching program cost. I was surprised; Lisa was shocked. He didn't try to close us on the first call. In fact, just the opposite. He knew that I had just closed on my HELOC weeks prior, and he wanted to make sure I was in a secure enough financial position to afford the cost of the program. I remember thinking that even though he had just met me, I could tell he really wanted to see me succeed.

At the end of our conversation, he asked us to think it over and scheduled another meeting. We had about a week and a half to talk about it and pray. Lisa and I felt the clock ticking, so we took this seriously as each day moved forward. This short timeline proved to be effective because we did not want to make the wrong decision. He used a technique called BAMFAM (book a meeting from a meeting), which is a tactic I have since implemented when cold calling myself.

As each day passed, I was convinced, but Lisa still needed more assurance. I value this about my wife, or at least I do now because at the time I was a bit annoyed. I'm the kind of person who tends to jump before I look, like I did with the HELOC, but she is there to remind me to strap on my parachute. As the meeting with Chris got closer, there wasn't a clear word from God for Lisa.

I grew impatient and a little agitated because I knew that this was the right move, but I refused to start this if we weren't in complete agreement. We prayed and prayed and prayed. We discussed it over and over, but the conversation always ended as indecisive as before. I feared that indecision would be our decision, which scared me the most because I didn't want to miss out on what I believed was God's will.

The morning of my meeting with Chris, Lisa was on her way to work, so I called to make one last pitch. She still was not sure. I figured I would have to ask Chris for more time, but honestly, there was something definite about this timeline. I knew that if we let today go by without starting the program, it would be the beginning of the end. The fire inside me could last only so long, and if we did not do this now, this dream would die. Before we got off the phone, I asked her to pray one more time. While it was stressful, frustrating, and angering in the moment, in retrospect, it was patience, peace, and trust in God developing in my life. I knew He spoke to me and was guiding me. Surely, He would not direct me on this path and forget to tell my wife. He knew this moment was coming for us both—a moment when Lisa and I were stretched beyond our capacity. Our faith was being tested and tried for such a time as this.

Alone in her car, she was praying out loud and seeking God for direction. As the words were coming out of her mouth, a car passed her. Written on the back window in bold white letters were the words,

To God be the Glory

That was the confirmation she needed. She finally knew God was behind this and that it would be for His glory, not ours. She called me immediately. With certainty in her voice, she said,

"Do it, and make sure you do it for God's glory."

I had my wife's support and God's confirmation. Now, there was nothing stopping me.

I was ready to get started immediately, and from my HELOC experience, I knew some things would have to change. I would have to change. As Daniel often says,

"The old you won't get new results."

Mindless social media distractions were replaced with real estate investment education. Watching a new show on Netflix was replaced with reading books on business and self-development. Instead of listening to music in the car, I would listen to podcasts about real estate. Email notifications became more important than Facebook notifications. Journaling became a daily ritual. Real estate meetups became more valuable than hanging out with friends. I knew what I did not know, but now I knew how to learn it. I got organized. I bought a briefcase and a portfolio. I carried my briefcase with a laptop, notepad, and whichever book I was currently reading back and forth to work. I endured the jest from coworkers because I was laser-focused. My downtime became business time. I spent my lunch hour on Zoom calls and blocked out time in my calendar to "build my empire." The only thing I was not willing to sacrifice was time that belonged to my family and God. Everything else needed an upgrade. I did not abandon any of my previous commitments; I just learned how to prioritize my time. My transformation was in full swing.

Step one was learning the course modules. I did not just watch them; I studied them. I took notes and then reviewed my notes. Then I watched them again. I developed my strategy and then revised my strategy. I attended every Zoom call in the program. I volunteered during conversational role-plays, not worrying about what I looked like because I knew that my value lay in taking action. I began reaching out to brokers and scheduling meetings with lawyers. I founded my company, Juniper Tree Investments LLC, and set up a website. I typed up a business plan and printed copies to hand out at meetings with potential investors. I built a business wardrobe to look the part. This was not a disguise; it was a transformation. I knew what I wanted in life, and I was determined to become the person capable of achieving it. This time I would not fizzle out. I was no longer reaching for success but, instead, creating an environment where success could thrive.

Everything I learned in that first month was building the confidence necessary to navigate the obstacles of real estate investing. If you want to achieve something you have never done, you have to become someone you have never been. You have to take a self-inventory of what is helping you achieve your goals and what is getting in the way. Next, decide if you are willing to make sacrifices for future returns. Just as we invest in real estate for the promise of future returns, you must invest in yourself. You have to be willing to strip away the shallow "comforts" of your current quality of life to make room for better-formed habits. Every mountaintop is at the bottom of the next mountain to climb, so if you find yourself uncomfortable, embrace it. There are no shortcuts to success. There are various scenarios that might make you wealthy by chance, but there is only one path to success. It is a long one littered with the corpses of those who gave up along the way. Success is inevitable for someone who is willing to keep putting one foot in front of the other no matter the circumstances. Failure only occurs once we have thrown in the towel. As long as we keep going, success is imminent. The reward is not the seven, eight, or nine-figure business but the transformation that takes place along the way. The mindset metamorphosis had begun.

In April of 2023, AREA held Mastermind in the Rockies in Colorado Springs, and I was eager to attend. I had heard raving reviews from last year's conference, and I was excited to meet everyone in person. While waiting in the airport lounge for my flight to board, I set up my laptop, opened the homepage of my website. I then placed my briefcase on a table next to a cup of coffee, and snapped a picture for Facebook. I added a caption that said,

Headed to Colorado Springs for Mastermind in the Rockies

This was a hard thing for me to do. It was out of character. I had never been a frequent poster on social media. I would normally scroll and look at other people's lives, but now I was starting a grassroots shout-from-the-rooftops marketing campaign. I decided I would tell everyone about my business; after all, if someone wanted to partner as an investor, they needed to know what I was doing first. I told everyone. Anyone who would listen. I became the "real estate guy." If someone was talking about interest rates, property values, or anything real estate-related, I inserted myself into their conversation. I had my strategy and pitch deck memorized. I spoke in absolutes. I never said, "I'm going to start a business." Instead, I said, "I run a business." Instead of, "I want to buy apartment buildings," I said, "I'm going to have 50 doors, and I'm going to raise $2 million in capital." I believe speaking in absolutes and telling people your goals not only builds confidence but also forces you to take action. Oftentimes when people start something new, they will keep it to themselves because if they fail, they can do so quietly. They are not afraid of failure as much as they are afraid of the judgment of their failures.

In 1951, Solomon Asch conducted what is known as the Asch Conformity Experiment. A test subject was seated at a table next to seven undercover participants posing as test subjects. All participants were asked to identify the correct answer to a series of problems and instructed to state each answer aloud one at a time. The unwitting test subject was seated last at the table and would hear everyone else's answer before providing his or her own. After answering the first few questions correctly, the undercover participants purposely began answering incorrectly. The basis of the experiment was to see if the test subject would give an answer they believed to be correct despite being the only one to do so. Would they speak out or conform?

The findings showed that 75% of test subjects purposely gave incorrect answers. They were willing to ignore what they knew to be true just to fit in. Would I be bold or fold under the pressures of conformity? From day one of my business, I have been loud and proud about my goals and ambition. If I fail, I risk public humiliation from the "I told you so" warriors, but when I succeed, I hope to do so with the people who cheered me on. When I step out on a ledge, even when everyone around me is shaken, I will take the leap.

When I arrived in Colorado Springs, my head was spinning. I freshened up from the flight in my hotel room and headed downstairs to meet fellow entrepreneurs at the Thursday night meet and greet. The Friday and Saturday sessions were filled with guest speakers, and it was transformative. Daniel jam-packed as much value into one weekend as possible. I used up three legal pads taking notes and soaked up an abundance of wisdom. I volunteered to sit in the hot seat in front of the audience and let Daniel poke holes in my business, of which there were plenty. Once it was finished, I left the event so jacked up that I could have flown home without the plane. That weekend was my baptism. It was not the knowledge gained but the mindset reframing that had the most impact. I had not yet achieved success, but we shared a meal. I sat across the table from success. The people I met had different stories, different backgrounds, and different paths, but they all shared a few things in common.

First, they invested in themselves. They measured success inwardly and tracked their transformation instead of their performance. Success, to them, was capability, not achievement. Achievement was the by-product of their inward transformation. They not only understood this principle but embraced it. I expected to hear stories about overcoming obstacles and testaments of grandeur; instead, they consistently reinforced the idea of personal development in their lives and the importance of implementing it in ours. You've heard the adage about giving a man a fish or teaching him how to fish. Well, they taught us how to select the best fishing pole, determine which bait to use, and find the best fishing spots in uncharted waters. It was a masterclass in professionalism.

They also shared a willingness to help other people by partnering with other professionals to achieve a goal. They didn't want to be the last person standing atop a conquered hill. Their desire was to fill the hilltop with the people who helped get them there. This was an atmosphere the Kwak brothers fostered. Their hearts have always been to help others succeed, and they filled their conference with like-minded success stories.

Finally, I noticed they all had an abundance mindset. A scarcity mindset believes there is a finite number of dollars, assets, and deals, leading to hoarding behaviors and habits. In contrast, an abundance mindset is one of inclusion and believes that all parties can benefit from any given transaction. These were the types of people I wanted to learn from. Hollywood tends to portray success as cutthroat and ruthless. They'll have you believe that the ladder to the top is made of people you need to step on to arrive. I couldn't disagree more. The best way to enjoy your success is by cultivating relationships, building trust, and growing together. Build an attractive reputation that precedes you, and the law of attraction takes effect. There's an old proverb that best sums up this philosophy:

If you want to travel fast, travel alone.
If you want to travel far, travel together.

The most memorable part of the weekend came Sunday morning during our last session. Daniel was giving us a few action items and said that he would love to have successful students as speakers at future events. I blurted out in a playfully sarcastic tone,

"Would you like to book me now?"

The room laughed, and Daniel appreciated my confidence. While disguised as a joke, deep down, I meant every word. I spoke it into existence. Seven months later, at Mastermind in the Oasis, I had a 45-minute speaking slot on raising capital. I left the conference a changed man, but now it was time to get to work.

GIVE ME SIX HOURS TO
CHOP DOWN A TREE, I'D
SPEND THE FIRST FOUR
SHARPENING THE AX.

———————————

ABRAHAM LINCOLN

CHAPTER THREE

SHARPENING THE AX

———— · ————————

Upon returning home, I had action items to follow, plans to implement, and goals to achieve. I felt like I had a better grasp on the industry now, as I began using the terminology and speaking their language. I was reviewing deals, putting in offers, practicing underwriting, and calculating CAP rates and NOI. I could project what the cash-on-cash return would be if I raised X amount for a purchase price of Y amount, minus expense ratio and debt service. I was honing my skills and sharpening my ax.

Something I learned from my mentors was that it was equally important to practice things I was bad at as much as the areas where I naturally excelled. I'm pretty good socially, so when I'm face-to-face with someone, I'm relaxed and presentable. When I'm on the phone, however, I come off as transactional and uncaring. I tend to talk a little too fast and get straight to the point. Chris, having a background in sales, often repeats,

> *"People don't care how much you know,*
> *until they know how much you care."*

On the phone, I don't come off as caring. I'm about as gentle as a bull in a china shop, so to fix this, I began to practice.

My training began by searching for a listed property that was far too expensive for me to purchase, and then I would submit a letter of intent (LOI). This gave me lots of opportunities to practice real-life scenarios and situations. I would calculate what the purchase price would be based on a 10% capitalization rate (CAP): the ratio between a property's Net Operating Income (NOI) and the purchase price. If a property was listed for $2 million and the CAP rate was 7%, I would offer $1.4 million, which would be a 10% CAP. I had no intention of purchasing the property at this point. I was practicing professional interactions. I would submit my offer via email and wait for a call from the broker. When the broker would call, he would usually tell me that his client wouldn't entertain that offer, but now we were on the phone, so phase two of my training began. I would start asking questions and engaging in conversation.

My goal was to stay on the phone for five minutes.

I used these phone calls as opportunities to try out different questions and approaches as I began to learn which ones resonated and which ones did not. Some questions moved the conversation forward, while others led to dead ends. I began developing the technique of asking open-ended questions, which led to much more information being divulged as opposed to a simple yes or no. Some of my favorites were, "How did the seller come up with that price?" or "It seems like a great property; why is he even selling?" These conversations started out choppy and uncomfortable, but over time they became pleasant and constructive.

I was also learning how to answer questions about my strategy and the types of properties I was looking for. During my first few interactions, my strategy was vague and unorganized, but as I continued to practice, I learned how to convey my strategy and articulate my goals. I also began to notice that as I got more specific, I came across as more professional to the broker, and in turn, he would take me more seriously. All this repetition was helping me hone my skills.

I spent a lot of time repeating this process and getting better each time. With each conversation, my ax got a little sharper. If you find yourself in the learning curve of a new skill, don't discount the importance of repetition. It can be easy to lose steam when practicing because we all yearn for results. I wanted results too, but I knew that practicing was making me better. Some days making the phone calls was difficult, and other days I felt like an imposter, but I pushed through and trusted the process.

After a few months of practicing professional interactions, I knew it was time to get serious, and in order to make serious offers, I would need money to put it under contract. Since I didn't have money of my own, I would have to raise money. But how? After joining Accelerated Real Estate Academy, I learned how to raise capital from limited partners. The limited partner invests his capital, and the general partner, i.e., the real estate investor, finds, negotiates, and closes the deal. The notion of asking people for money struck incredible fear into me. It reminded me of when I first got certified to scuba dive. After all the instructions and skill tests, you still have to get out of the boat for the first time. In that moment, suited up, masked up, and seated on the edge of the boat, you know everything you need to know, but still, all the fear rushes back and tries to dissuade you from diving in. Then, you dive.

At the heart of any pitch, the investor is not investing in your deal; he is investing in you. So I asked myself a simple question: "Would I give myself money?" If my answer is no, then what would I have to do to become that person? I would have to believe that an investor's money is safer with me than with them. Recently, the ice maker in the freezer started making a weird noise and wouldn't dispense ice or water. Fixing the ice maker is not in my wheelhouse, so my money is better spent on getting a professional I trust to fix it for me. Therefore, I trust my money is in better hands with an ice maker repairman. Likewise, if I've invested in myself enough to become an expert concerning the subject matter of real estate investing, then someone who is not a real estate professional has a better chance investing with me than doing it alone. With the knowledge I've gained and contacts I've made, I could confidently tell myself that I was a safer option. It was imperative that I believed it, or no one else would.

Daniel announced that for the month of June, we were tasked with a capital-raising challenge. The rules were simple: whoever was able to raise the most capital with signed letters of verbal agreement by midnight on June 30th was the winner. He was pretty adamant that all submissions had to be in before midnight CST. The winner would get a trip to his office in Chicago, a plug on his podcast, and courtside seats at a Bulls game. This was the catalyst that motivated me to take action.

Part of the groundwork for raising capital had already been laid by telling everyone that I was now a real estate investor. My pitch deck was always on the tip of my tongue. When I flew, I wore a suit and flew first class because business professionals fly first class. I purposely booked flights with layovers to maximize my interactions. I struck up conversations with passengers next to me and even talked to people in the airport lounges. In everyday life, I would introduce myself as a real estate investor and always handed out business cards. My military career had become my side gig; now, I was a real estate investor.

As I learned with raising capital, preparation is key. Being prepared will alleviate any self-doubt. Don't take this lightly. Whether you're giving a pitch to raise capital, making a presentation at work, or trying to close a deal, make sure you prepare the right way. Take the time necessary to formulate your thoughts. Imagine how the pitch will go and look for holes. Practice in the mirror and role-play with an associate because any pitch, presentation, or negotiation will never go according to plan. At some point, you will be asked a question you didn't anticipate, or something will be said that throws you off track. In these moments, you need to be quick on your feet and have the ability to pivot. Much like a jazz musician can improvise because he has first learned the fundamentals, you will only be able to pivot because you've spent time in preparation. Once you learn the rules like a professional, you can break them like an artist.

Three days into the capital-raising challenge, I was discussing a possible deal with a friend. This person dabbled in real estate and had just sold a single-family home, but he had no exposure to multifamily buildings or apartments. I simply showed him the deal and mentioned that I would have to raise about $130,000 to make the purchase. I was still waiting for more information on the specifics of the property, but I was at least interested. Over the course of just a few minutes, I explained what I knew about the deal so far and what a partnership with me would look like, and surprisingly, he offered me the money. That was all it took. There was no slideshow, no boardrooms, and no meetings. It was just a conversation—a conversation between friends that led to a verbal commitment for $130,000.

As the following days' events unfolded, the deal proved to no longer be a sound investment. After a few more conversations with my investor, we decided we weren't right for a partnership. There was no animosity or ill will; it just wasn't the right fit. You may think I was crazy for terminating a partnership with an investor, but this is where I learned my most valuable lesson about raising capital: no amount of money is worth working with the wrong partner.

Partnerships are like marriages. They are built on trust and transparency, and they cost a lot of money to dissolve. When listening to presentations about raising capital, I was warned about the dangers of getting into the wrong partnership, but I told myself, "There's no way I'm turning down money." Well, I was wrong. In this case, it became clear that our goals weren't aligned. He liked the idea of fixing and flipping properties, whereas my strategy was to buy and hold them. He was more interested in an area of town I wanted to avoid. I was more focused on building equity over time while he just wanted immediate cash flow. These are all things that should be established before a partnership is formed. In short, I walked away from $130,000 and what would have probably been a huge mistake. Thankfully, I was able to learn these lessons without paying the price. If life offers me a free lesson, then I'll learn it the first time.

Everything I had learned about raising capital

was true, and this was a skill I was capable of mastering. Each call was terrifying, but when I finally did something right, it was exhilarating. It reminded me of my first few rounds of golf. While 98% of my round was a disaster, the only thing I remembered was the shot that could have been a highlight on ESPN. Those are the shots that keep me coming back. Over the next few months, I had several interactions with potential investors. Some would close while others would not, so I kept track of when I hit the mark as well as what might have caused me to derail. With each interaction, regardless of the outcome, my confidence was building, and my ax was sharper than ever. I did not win the capital-raising challenge, but I elevated my skill enough to cause Daniel to entrust me with presenting at his event. The challenge may have ended, but my capital-raising journey was just beginning.

The reason I found success with raising capital was that I approached it meticulously and was determined to understand its underlying principles. While every pitch for capital is unique, at the heart of every fundraiser are the same fundamentals: faith and trust, or fear and skepticism. If you've ever had someone pitch you a multilevel marketing pyramid scheme, you can probably remember how uncomfortable that conversation made you feel. Skepticism is the manifestation of your deeply rooted fears. While you may be skeptical of the product, you're really afraid of entrusting your money with someone else. When giving a pitch, it's important to understand what your counterpart is feeling. This will help you navigate the conversation and avoid triggering their fears. The best tool to successfully overcome fear is faith. When someone has enough faith in you to suppress their fear, that is the foundation of a good partnership.

Leading up to the Mastermind in the Oasis, I had raised over one million in capital and was offered the opportunity to share my success with the clients in attendance. I was honored that Daniel entrusted me with speaking at his event, and I didn't take it lightly. I approached it like raising capital; I took no shortcuts in my preparation. I imagined myself in the audience, then I crafted a presentation to cut through fear and skepticism. Instead of getting them to commit money, my goal was to get them to commit themselves. I truly believed in what I was selling, and I wanted them to believe they were capable as well. It was an amazing experience. At my first mastermind, I was wide-eyed and eager to learn. Seven months later, I was presenting to the group. That, in itself, was a huge achievement for me. Daniel gave me another shot of encouragement before I left. He said,

"Next time, I want you to share on closing a deal."

WHEN YOU HIT A WRONG
NOTE, IT'S THE NEXT NOTE
THAT DETERMINES IF IT'S
GOOD OR BAD.

———————————

MILES DAVIS

CHAPTER FOUR

WIND AND HAIL

——— · ———

In real estate, several different methods exist to find deals. Searching for listings on the MLS, calling "for rent" signs, cold calling property owners, and attending networking events are a few examples. As with any profession, networking is of extreme importance. It is usually advantageous to be in the same room with like-minded individuals because you never know what opportunities may arise. Networking events or meetups for real estate investors are often held during the week. Even though it was physically exhausting to attend these events and then work the next day, I couldn't ignore the value of meeting people who had walked in my shoes. One day, at a real estate investor meetup, I met a wholesaler with whom I would sign a contract to purchase 31 units in Houma, LA.

To briefly explain, wholesaling involves bringing

off-market deals to buyers. A wholesaler will cold call the owner of a property valued at $180,000. They negotiate and agree on a purchase price (e.g., $150,000) and sign a contract. Next, the wholesaler finds an "end buyer" and negotiates a new purchase price (e.g., $170,000). The wholesaler then "assigns" the contract to the end buyer and walks away with the $20,000 difference for brokering the deal.

After making this connection, I wasted no time negotiating a contract to purchase 31 units for $2.2 million with a $200,000 kickback at closing. The property performed well, and I finally felt like I was about to hit a home run. As soon as I signed the contract, I had a rush of adrenaline that wouldn't cease for the next two weeks. I had a 14-day due diligence period during which I would conduct walkthroughs and inspections, verify expenses, and secure funding. A year ago, I was stressed over the obstacles of my HELOC, but now I welcomed the challenges of closing on 31 units. All of my preparation had led up to this point. Nothing was going to stop me from closing on this deal.

I began hitting obstacles immediately. First, I spoke with multiple lenders. When trying to acquire a loan of this size, the lender requires a personal financial statement. Mine is far from impressive because I do not have any real assets besides my primary residence and my one rental. Most banks turned me down from the get-go, but eventually, I found a lender willing to underwrite the loan. I wasn't in a position to negotiate terms, so I was now facing an interest rate above the market rate.

At first glance, one might say that 2023 was not the best year to purchase real estate. The economy was still recovering from COVID-19 lockdowns, and interest rates were rising to heights we hadn't seen since 1980. Inflation was devaluing the dollar, and the cost of money was causing many investors to watch from the sidelines. Additionally, we were seeing poor strategies from amateur investors being exposed. Warren Buffett famously said, "Only when the tide goes out do you learn who has been swimming naked." That is a perfectly accurate illustration of the 2023 real estate landscape. Amateur investors were getting caught skinny-dipping as financial institutions across the country were draining the pool and ultimately causing a record number of foreclosures and portfolios to be sold at a loss. Thankfully, in the midst of a fairly unstable financial climate, the numbers still worked, so I pushed forward.

Next, we conducted the walkthrough. I found

that four of the units were in the middle of a complete remodel and would cost approximately $100,000 to complete. This meant I'd be spending an extra $100,000 with no rent coming in until the remodels were finished. While this may have been problematic, I had secured a $200,000 kickback at closing, so I would be able to stabilize the property and finish the renovations. I was still on track.

My next step was to verify expenses. It is important to not only calculate what the current owner is paying but also include the cost of maintaining the property. This is when I uncovered what would be my coup de grâce: the final blow. Ever since Hurricane Ida impacted the Louisiana Gulf Coast in September 2021, property insurance skyrocketed. I noticed the current owner didn't have a wind and hail policy. I called multiple insurance agents to get quotes, and it soon became clear that promising returns could easily turn into major losses.

My deadline was approaching, and I faced a crucial decision. Imposter syndrome started to creep in and cause self-doubt. I felt I was in over my head as the waters continued to rise. If I backed out of this deal, I would lose face with my investors and mentors. If I went through with the deal, I might be overextended and vulnerable. The numbers were so tight that I would be heavily relying on factors beyond my control. I would be hoping that interest rates and insurance costs would go down. Even replacing one air conditioning unit could put me under. With the stress mounting, the risks multiplying, and the deadline approaching, I made the hardest decision I'd ever made in my real estate career.

I TERMINATED THE CONTRACT

The loss of that deal struck a tremendous blow to my confidence. For the first time since starting this business, I considered throwing in the towel. I had to decide whether to accept failure and return to normality or to take the lessons learned and apply them moving forward. My motivation was on life support. Giving up seemed so easy. I hadn't lost anyone's money, and I still had my W-2 income. I could walk away, and my life would remain unchanged.

It was during these moments of self-doubt that I truly transformed into a real estate investor. When faced with such a significant disappointment, I had to be honest with myself. Was I really an entrepreneur, or had I just looked the part? Were my business cards worth the paper they were printed on? Everything I had done to tweak my personality and consciously improve meant nothing if it never led to results. If I walked away now, would all of this be for naught?

New characteristics that I had not previously possessed started to emerge. After all I had gone through to reach this moment, who was I kidding? No matter what I did next, I was forever changed. The question was, what would I do with the obstacles in front of me? The past version of me gave up, and it took Lisa's encouragement to get back into it, but this was even too big for her. I needed guidance and realignment, so I booked a trip to Chicago to meet with Daniel at his office.

Just the act of going to Chicago was a step in the right direction. This was the first time I had been to Daniel's office. Keeping to my routine, I flew in a suit and booked a layover. I looked like a real estate investor, but inside I felt like an imposter. Taking a tour of the office, I began to feel my motivation rising once again. I figured this guy was a broke college kid, and look at him now. He and his brother run eight businesses from their office. I felt like I was looking at my future. After the tour, Daniel sat down with me to discuss my business.

Daniel has a unique ability to cut through all the fluff and identify your choke points. He showed me what I was doing right and areas that needed improvement. Even though I had just had a deal fall through, he had not lost any confidence in me. In the midst of this whirlwind, as I struggled to determine if I had made the right decision, Daniel looked me in the eyes and said,

"Because you walked away from that deal, this is my proudest moment as your mentor. You made the right choice. Although it was hard, I couldn't be prouder."

When I was heading to Chicago, I was discouraged but hopeful. By the time I left, I was determined and steely-eyed. I wasn't a fraud. I hadn't failed. I stayed professional and didn't let emotions cloud my judgment. I chose logic over emotions and didn't let the wind and hail surrounding me extinguish my fire. I walked away and lived to tell the tale, but now it was time to get back to work and secure my first deal.

YOU CAN'T WIN IN LIFE IF
YOU'RE LOSING IN YOUR
MIND. CHANGE YOUR
THOUGHTS AND YOU'LL
CHANGE YOUR LIFE.

———————————

TONY GASKINS

CHAPTER FIVE

A DEFINABLE WIN

———— · ————

When a business runs smoothly, a deal falling through should not affect momentum. It shouldn't depend on closing deals. Instead, it needs to be constantly engaged in deals to be most effective. For example, NFL teams with only one star receiver often struggle to spread the ball evenly or establish the run. Opposing defensive squads focus on shutting down that one receiver, which can cripple the entire offense. The best offensive units spread the ball evenly, making them unpredictable to the defense. They are often more productive and successful because of this approach. My business was suffering from similar issues. I had invested all my energy in one deal, but I had neglected to strategize effectively. I had placed my perception of success on closing this deal, so once it fell through, I was back at square one. I needed to shift my focus toward the process, making deals the byproduct of a sustainable business model. Daniel calls this the acquisition process.

To effectively implement an acquisition process, I first needed to zoom out and gain a broader perspective. What does it take to close one deal? To close on **one** property, I would need **three** properties under contract. Having three properties under contract means I would need to negotiate with **ten**. To have that many negotiations, I would need **25** owners to consider selling. If only one out of four owners would consider selling, then I would need to contact **100** property owners. That means, theoretically, **100** cold calls equals **one deal**. This drastically altered my perspective because my focus had been in the wrong place. The best way to climb a mountain is one step at a time, but I had been focused on the peak instead of the next step. If I learn to blaze the trail, the summits will come. I took the blinders off and could now see the field for what it was. I had to trust the process and do the work.

A crucial part of implementing new processes is keeping metrics to track what is working versus what is not. With the ability to refer back to data, I was now able to evaluate each part of my process and improve the weak points. The weakest part for me was the initial contact: cold calling. Since roughly 100 cold calls are required for one deal, I could no longer afford to avoid them. As painful as cold calling may be, these leads were the lifeblood of the process. It was important that these calls were converting as well. I could call 100 people, but if my pitch was faulty, I wouldn't convert any of them. Therefore, I began making calls, tracking the data, correcting my mistakes, and repeating the process.

Another metric I needed to track was myself. At Mastermind in the Rockies in April 2023, we all took the Culture Index survey. The survey was a personality test that measures work-related traits. The results placed us into three separate categories, showing each of us our strengths and weaknesses while also revealing which categories we flex into, our underlying motivator, and the severity of each trait from moderate to extreme. Here, I learned how to study the metrics of my personality.

For those unfamiliar with these specific tests, you might better define me as a "trailblazer" because I have always been outgoing and confident. The survey also categorized me as "extremely autonomous" and pinpointed my motivation to compete and win. The advantages were that I am both ambitious and capable, which explains my headstrong nature. I'm the "big picture" person who attacks every task with a "by any means necessary" attitude. On the flip side, whenever I am forced to do something, my weaknesses start to show. The tension and stress of having to do something instead of wanting to often cause me to abandon it entirely. I begin to lose interest and give little to no effort. This did not surprise me much since I have started multiple projects in the past that I left unfinished. It's not a proud character trait, but it doesn't have to define or cripple me from achieving my goals. It takes an internal and continual drive to keep moving forward. I can't afford to "not feel like it" one day. I have to constantly strive, day in and day out, to make my dreams a reality.

Worst of all, the survey revealed that one of my greatest weaknesses is thinking I can do it all on my own. I often wore this as a badge of pride, believing I am self-sufficient and don't need to ask for help or guidance. I can do whatever I put my mind to. However, the independent mindset can lead many astray as they struggle to accomplish anything.

Seeing these negative tendencies on paper made me reevaluate myself. I didn't want to be a victim of myself or be the obstacle in my way. Daniel told me that he loves to mentor "autonomous" students because they often take action, but he rarely gets the chance because they usually decide they can do it by themselves. I was so close to closing that previous deal, and it would have been on my own, but it would have come at a great cost. Thankfully, I avoided that struggle by partnering with mentors and heeding their guidance. It is crucial to resist the innate urge to go it alone and, instead, lean on those wiser and more experienced around you.

> *"If you're the smartest person in the room, you're in the wrong room." - Jack Welch*

It is essential to assess yourself. Each person has personality traits that will hinder their progress, and no one is smart enough to do it alone. The real estate industry will challenge each weakness, no matter what your personality type is, and if you are not prepared, it will crush you. There is so much involved and too much at stake to think you will not be stretched to capacity. Some days, tasks will be right inside your wheelhouse, while other days, the workload in front of you will make you doubt yourself and question whether or not you even belong here. Just know that until you reach the end of your first deal, you are faking it. You don't have the skills needed to handle multiple deals. You have no experience, and you never will until you get started. You will fail if you rely on natural instincts and raw talent alone. This is not a one-man band; it is an orchestra. It's an ensemble with precise choreography. Each step must be calculated and unwavering. Real estate investing will take unparalleled focus and determination.

The good news is that many have stood where you stand now. Whether you are on the brink of your first deal or have yet to get started, many successful individuals have been there too. They worked extremely hard to get where they wanted, and so can you. It takes courage and tenacity, but those who are scared beyond belief and take action despite the uncertainty around them are showing true bravery. When you find yourself terrified of the situations at hand, don't let circumstances and setbacks discourage you. Embrace each hardship and know that you are being forged in fire. It is in these moments that true bravery is born.

Another skill set I had yet to master was negotiating. The last thing I wanted was to find myself sitting across from an agent as they stared daggers at me and proceeded to negotiate circles around me.

"Everybody has a plan until you get punched in the mouth." - Mike Tyson

Mike Tyson often said that when he looked at his opponents across the ring, he could see the fear in their eyes. They lost the fight before it even started. He spent countless hours working, training, and becoming the scariest guy in the red corner imaginable, and it paid off. His dedication and preparation made him a formidable opponent. Once he looked into their eyes, he knew the fight was over. If I had any chance of succeeding in this industry, I had to become a fierce negotiator. I had to train consistently so that when I began negotiating for real multimillion dollar properties, I would be ready. This posed a dilemma: I only had so much time to spend making cold calls and negotiating, so I had to begin outsourcing work.

I knew negotiating would be crucial for me to learn, so I began researching the best ways to outsource cold calling. First, I would have to find someone I trusted to make calls on my behalf. I could hire a virtual assistant and provide a list of property owners and phone numbers, but this option wouldn't offer an incentive to convert leads. My second option was to ask a family member or friend, but I worried that the lack of industry knowledge would result in suboptimal results. The best option was to find a young and eager Realtor who would jump at the chance to practice making calls while earning a commission simultaneously. Realtors are accustomed to doing work upfront for payment in the future, and they would certainly have the understanding, terminology, and professionalism needed to engage in these conversations. In turn, I would get the leads I needed, allowing me to focus on negotiating.

In his book, *Never Split the Difference*, Chris Voss, a former FBI negotiator, teaches how to relate to your counterpart using something called "tactical empathy." The trick is to ignore your own preconceptions and meet the other person on common ground. I began to look inwardly to reassess my motives, and my conversations began to take on a different tone. I was no longer leveraging a relationship to benefit my needs but instead trying to offer value in any way I could. Instead of imposing my will, I would genuinely inquire about their needs and struggles. It was less about whether I could get a good deal and more about whether we were a good fit.

In October 2023, I met with an owner at her six-unit building in an upscale part of town. This lead came from cold calling property owners in the area. She was a sweet lady in her mid-70s who had inherited the property years before. Her father had purchased the building when she was only seven years old, for what I imagine cost less than a new vehicle today. There hadn't been a mortgage in years, and she lived in the largest apartment in the back of the building. It seemed to have the potential to be my first deal. I had practiced my negotiating tactics, and now it was time to use them. I wanted to be confident, well-versed, and knowledgeable, but more importantly, I wanted her to think the same. I wasn't quite sure what to expect, but once I arrived, I noticed she wasn't alone.

Her son had flown in from Houston for our meeting because he was afraid I was an institutional developer swooping in to steamroll his elderly mother. I can't blame him; I'm sure I would have done the same. Unfortunately, there are many wolves looking to prey upon the weak. I was nothing of the sort, and I never intend to be. I want to stay true to myself as a Christian and do this for the glory of God. I cannot, in good conscience, build wealth at the expense of good people. I have to remember that I am actually looking out for them just as much, if not more, whether it benefits me or not. They invited me in, introduced themselves, and before we even had a chance to speak, he quickly made his purpose for being there clear.

"What is your intention in wanting to purchase this property?"

I was completely caught off guard. This wasn't how I expected the conversation to start. I replied,

"First, let me introduce myself,
and tell you what I'm trying to accomplish."

I explained my strategy and told them that I had just started in the industry. I mentioned that I was hoping to build a portfolio of rental properties. Normally, I would be asking more questions than verbalizing my biography, but I sensed he was afraid. Here I was, negotiating for the first time since changing my motives, so I reminded myself: it's about whether we are a good fit.

"I appreciate you being here to prevent someone from
trying to take advantage of your mother."

He exhaled and sat back in his chair as the tension left the room. It was as if someone had opened a window and let a cool breeze in. We could all breathe a sigh of relief as we continued our discussion. He was relieved to know I wasn't a vulture looking to take advantage. After a tour of the property and reviewing the rent roll and a price they were comfortable with, I spoke with him privately. I explained that while the property was in a great location, his mother had not increased rents for years, so all the units were severely under market value. If I were to make an offer based on the current rates, I wouldn't be able to pay what she deserved. Furthermore, I would have to nearly double the rent if I did, and in turn, I would be evicting her elderly tenants, which is not what either of us wanted. I suggested they incrementally raise the rent over the next few years to bring the property to market at a fair price. He sincerely thanked me for my time and advice and promised that when they were serious about selling, I would be the first person they called.

This is not the story of how I closed my first deal, but it's a definable win. I've gone over that conversation a hundred times in my mind, and I think about how it was a major step in the direction I want to go. I ignored self-interest in favor of the interest of others by softening my transactional nature and providing value with nothing in return. Hopefully, they take my advice, strengthen their position, and call me back when they're ready to sell. But even if that call never comes, the change in my perspective is the win that keeps me moving forward.

THE MIRACLE ISN'T THAT I
FINISHED. THE MIRACLE IS
THAT I HAD THE COURAGE
TO START.

———————————

JOHN BINGHAM

CHAPTER SIX

THE WALL

———————— · ————————

The pieces were falling into place, and my business was taking shape. As my network grew, I was sure that results were close, but I was struggling mentally because I really thought I would have a deal by now. Sure, the market was less than favorable, and I expected there would be challenges and obstacles, but I hadn't anticipated how much sowing would be required before I would get to reap some success. It's one thing to read inspirational stories, but walking it out in real time is not for the faint of heart. Everyone dreams of being Michael Jordan hitting a buzzer beater, but how many have the discipline to practice that shot thousands of times? When runners take on a marathon, spectators gather around the finish line to applaud, but the accomplishment isn't at the finish line. It's at mile 20: *the wall.*

Marathon runners often refer to mile 20 as the wall or the dreaded mile. It's the point in the race where their body starts to shut down and refuses to continue. Most runners quit at this point in the race, but those who power through ignore their body's plea to stop. Through mental fortitude, they force their bodies to bend to their will. Their desire to complete the race overpowers their pain. They don't ignore the pain but embrace it. Their goal is no longer reaching the finish line but overcoming the next step.

At this point in my real estate journey, I was hitting a wall, but what felt like an isolated struggle was more prevalent than I thought. I noticed other entrepreneurs from AREA had stopped showing up to the Zoom calls, and I began seeing new faces every week. The people who were once engaged in the program were nowhere to be found. When they hit their wall, the lack of discipline caused them to drop out because they were focused on the results rather than taking it one step at a time. I was once the new guy eager to learn from veteran clients, but suddenly, I was a veteran of the group. We all know the program works because the clients who stay on course achieve success, but those who don't stay actively committed to the process fall by the wayside. The truth is, people are willing to invest money but aren't willing to invest in themselves.

For runners, the point at which self-doubt creeps in is when the voice in their head is loudest. The finish line is not in sight as they continue miles away from the cheering crowd, and their only companions are the competitors around them and themselves. It's when they are alone and can no longer hear external encouragement that the truest test of mental fortitude begins. The battle fought between the brain and the body happens in isolation after the motivation that fueled the beginning of the race diminishes. The only outside feedback is the runners next to them dropping out, but there comes a point where the runner begins to feel he may be next.

It's during the wall that you've got to decide if you'll become a casualty or ignore every excuse to stop, regardless of the pain in your body. With every muscle tightening and screaming for relief, the runner must crucify his flesh and conquer his mind if he has any chance of finishing the race. There comes a point where you can't fake it anymore because there are no shortcuts to success. The most arduous part of the journey usually occurs right before the breakthrough. It's up to the journeyman to continue. It's the decision of the runner to push through the wall, and it's during the dreaded mile where you find out what you're really made of.

In Napoleon Hill's *Think and Grow Rich*, he tells a story called "Three Feet from Gold." A man headed west in search of gold. After finding a small vein of gold, he went back home and raised money to purchase machinery in hopes of following the vein to a larger gold deposit. After weeks of drilling, the vein unexpectedly stopped, and there was still no gold in sight. He was discouraged after spending weeks working, only to end up short. So he sold the machinery to a junkyard owner and headed back east. The man recounted his failed venture when he sold the machinery to the junkyard owner. After hearing the man's story, the junkyard owner hired a mining expert and returned to the site to pick up where the man left off. As it turns out, the man had given up only three feet from gold. I read *Think and Grow Rich* in the first months of starting my business, and I promised myself that I wouldn't give up three feet away from gold. Even if I miscalculated my timeline to success, I would keep pressing on.

> *"Success is the ability to go from failure to failure without losing enthusiasm." -Winston Churchhill*

Some days, repeating that quote aloud in the mirror was the only enthusiasm I could muster as

I continued my journey in the trenches. No matter how hard it was, I continued showing up to meetings, reviewing the modules, and underwriting deals. I just kept going.

The hardest part of my dreaded mile was the feeling that I'd done everything necessary to avoid the wall. I hired a coach, implemented action items, learned the material and knowledge necessary to execute deals, and even walked away from a potential misstep, which was very hard to do. I prioritized relationships over transactions, raised capital, transformed my mindset, and followed the formula, yet I had nothing to show for it. I thought back to Daniel's book. After following the action steps from his coaches and mentors, Daniel was frustrated with his lack of progress, but he overcame his wall during his daily Bible reading where God showed him his next step. My wife told me from the beginning, "Do it for the glory of God," so it was time to go back to the source.

My next action item didn't come from modules, inspirational quotes, or a book; it came from spending time in prayer. I prayed and asked God what was hindering my progress, and He showed me that I was relying on my own strength instead of relying on Him. I was pushing and pushing but was running out of energy as I approached the wall. Everything I had done up to this point was necessary, but now it was time to let God carry me through.

God told me to start thanking Him for the success I had yet to achieve, so that's what I did. I started by thanking Him for closing on what would be my first deal and for allowing me to step into my call to fulfill my purpose. I thanked Him for facilitating the change in me and bringing the right people into my life. I was no longer trying to fulfill my will but His.

> *"But they that wait upon the Lord shall renew their strength; they shall mount up with wings as eagles; they shall run, and not be weary; and they shall walk, and not faint." Isaiah 40:31*

Once I started to reframe my desire, I was no longer bothered by my current circumstance, and that dreaded mile didn't feel quite as long. I was no longer crippled by self-imposed pressures because I didn't have to rely on my own energy. God was giving me the stamina I needed. No longer was I running this race alone. God was with me every step of the way.

Learning to wait on God was the theme for the next few months; not just in my real estate journey, but also in my personal life. Our daughter was turning three, and Lisa and I were ready for a second child, but after months of trying, we started to get discouraged. We were praying for God to give us the desires of our heart, but He was teaching us to truly rely on Him. This time of testing brought us closer together and closer to God. In the midst of approaching a wall in real estate, our family was facing a wall as well. This was a season of stretching for us, but God is greater than the trials manifesting around us. Lisa really wanted me to have a boy. I spent years of my life ministering to boys through a church program called Royal Rangers, and she wanted me to have the chance to share that experience with our son. We had our girl, and she is our princess, so now we wanted a son to round out our little family. We clung to the hope that God would fulfill our desire as Lisa started to pray the prayer of Hannah from the book of 1 Samuel. Hannah was barren and wanted to conceive a child, so she prayed in the temple and promised to dedicate her child to the Lord. The Bible tells us that God heard her prayer, and she gave birth to Samuel, who eventually became the spiritual leader of Israel.

One Sunday at church, someone told us that God had heard our prayers and Lisa would concieve that month. We received it as a promise from God and continued to pray. That month, we prayed and believed, but as each day went by, we still had no confirmation. Soon, the month ended, and many people around us began to wonder. Was God truly speaking to us or were we confused and misled? Lisa and I refused to accept that and continued to believe. It wasn't until halfway through the next month that we had a positive pregnancy test. God kept His promise because Lisa was pregnant the month before, but we only had confirmation afterward. When we found out it was a boy, we decided to name him Samuel. God's promises are always fulfilled, but in His timing, not ours.

I FIND I'M SO EXCITED,
I CAN BARELY SIT STILL
OR HOLD A THOUGHT IN
MY HEAD. I THINK IT'S
THE EXCITEMENT ONLY
A FREE MAN CAN FEEL,
A FREE MAN AT THE
START OF A JOURNEY
WHOSE CONCLUSION IS
UNCERTAIN.

———————————

RED, THE SHAWSHANK REDEMPTION

CHAPTER SEVEN

A GOOD FIT

———— · ————

One Monday morning, I woke up and started my day as usual. Mondays are a day off from work for me, so typically, I'd take my daughter to school on those days. I dressed in a pair of slacks and a polo shirt, gathered my briefcase and my daughter's belongings, and off we went. I turned on Christian music while she was pleasantly chatty the entire way. I even asked her what she thought Daddy did for work, to which she replied, "You make phone calls." It seemed she was right for the time being. My life had become a series of cold calls and networking, but I couldn't seem to gain reasonable traction. I felt I was in a funk and needed a change in perspective.

Weeks prior, during a lunch meeting with a broker/investor, I had received some valuable advice. He suggested that instead of waiting for the perfect deal to fall into my lap, I should consider deals I would usually dismiss and begin searching for listings first thing each morning. After dropping Lila off, I headed to a nearby coffee shop to get some work done. As I sat at the table, café au lait in hand, I opened my laptop and started searching for listings.

While scrolling through the MLS, I discovered a listing within the first two hours of hitting the market. The numbers on the offering memorandum looked very promising. I had seen plenty of listings like this before, and they often turned out to be too good to be true, but I called the listing agent anyway to get more information. Knowing that agents are often busy in meetings or showing properties, I left a message when no one answered. I like to note how quickly I get a call back because it tells me a bit about their work ethic and motivation to sell the property. If I have to call multiple times before getting a response, I can expect inconsistent behavior throughout the entire purchasing process. Additionally, whenever I leave messages, I purposely give out very little information about myself and speak quickly to create the impression that I'm busy and have other calls to make. Since this is his first impression of me, I want to sound professional, productive, and concise, giving the impression that I am an experienced investor.

During any professional interaction, it's important to pay attention to all the nuances in the conversation. When clients sign up for AREA, Daniel prepares them to perform at a higher skill level to compensate for their lack of experience. The goal is to perform as if it's our tenth deal by the time we enter our first deal.

The year spent immersed in real estate investment, equipped with knowledge from multiple modules, weekly Zoom calls, and countless books, has prepared me for these moments. That's why dressing the part, carrying a briefcase, introducing myself as a real estate investor, and using these tactics is so imperative. With zero deals to my name, this is how I cut through the noise and elevate myself as an experienced investor. This is where all the practice starts to pay off. All the clunky and awkward phone calls have become smooth and professional. The repetition of practice has brought me to a place where I can now have a productive conversation. Instead of worrying about how I sound, I listen for clues in the broker's response. Like a skilled musician, he listens and responds to the music rather than focusing on the shape of his chords. He isn't distracted by a lack of ability because he put in the work, and so have I.

He called back within the hour, which was a good

sign. When I answered the phone, I said,

"Are you calling me back about the 12 units in Metairie?"
He replied,

"No, I'm calling about the 18 unit deal in New Orleans."

    I referenced the wrong property on purpose to let him know I'm actively looking at other properties. To be honest, the first time I did this while speaking with an agent weeks prior, I referenced the wrong property by accident. When it happened, I noticed that his tone changed. Initially dismissive, he began to take me seriously when I mentioned another property. Suddenly, he thought he was talking to an experienced investor. From one sentence, I was able to present a portfolio of experience in his mind because people perceive things based on the evidence provided. After observing this effect, my goal moving forward was to recreate that perception in every interaction. It's not a trick; it's a persona. One that speaks for me and opens doors that might otherwise remain shut. I said,

"Oh right, those are the units that were listed earlier this morning, correct?"

"Yes, that's right. My name is Cameron Griffin, and I am

the listing agent for these properties. Thanks for giving me a call. So did you have any questions concerning the units?"

One thing I've learned is never to assume why someone is doing what they are doing. The last thing I want is to make a decision based on presumed reasons, so asking questions is important. Is there any current debt on the property? How long has the current owner had the units? When was the last time he raised the rents? Why is he selling them? How did he determine the purchase price? Questions like these help determine the seller's motivations, the property's condition, the best approach to financing the deal, and the likelihood of the deal being well-suited for me. If he said the seller wants to retire and the property is already paid off, then I know he's a good candidate for seller financing. If he wants to buy a bigger property, then I know I will have to use a lender. If he is moving out of state, then a quick sale will be more important to him than price, but if he based the price on what he paid for it, then he is emotionally attached, making negotiating the price harder.

As it turns out, the seller owned the asset for 20 years and wanted to buy a bigger property. He set the purchase price based on an appraisal from a year earlier when he nearly sold the property, but the sale fell through. This means I would need a lender for this property, but thankfully, he's probably not attached emotionally. Once I hung up the phone, I knew time was of the essence. I was ahead of the competition, so I began underwriting immediately.

The initial underwriting process involves examining broad numbers and making general assumptions to determine if the deal is worth pursuing further. While there is more involved, the main purpose is to decide if it's best to move forward. When underwriting a potential deal, I look for something called "headroom." I need to consider the cost versus profit margin to verify if this deal will work. When a sale takes place, property taxes and a new insurance policy are major costs to factor in. Additionally, due to market conditions, I know my interest rate will be higher than his current rate. Plus, I have to consider the cost of running the property. With all that in mind, I calculated a purchase price with enough headroom to enter the deal. The current listing price was $1,625,000. Full stop.

How many of you are immediately stressed? When you see that seventh digit, the million-dollar digit, things get serious. Remember, just a few chapters ago, I was overwhelmed by a HELOC. Many of you may have given up chapters ago, but some of you are holding out. Unfortunately, I lost half of you when you read that number. For those still reading, do not let this number scare you. This number represents everything you want in life. By no means am I saying that money is the source of happiness, but it does represent value. That's all it was ever meant to represent. The larger the number, the greater the value.

For those of you who are still here, you aren't giving up just yet because you know you have value. You have what it takes to work hard and achieve success at this level. Making a deal of this magnitude has always been this hard because only those with valuable work ethics are worthy of it. It's nothing more than a shift in mindset that moves the needle. We condition ourselves to believe we are not worthy of success. The transformation takes place when you start believing that success is within your grasp.

I knew I could offer $1,500,000 and still cover added expenses and debt service, so the next step was to submit a Letter of Intent (LOI). I typed up an LOI offering $1.5 million with a 30-day due diligence period and a subsequent 45 days to close. Now, I wait. My offer was low and ran the risk of insulting him, but I did my calculations and presented an offer that was fair and honest. Being the first to make an offer meant that he might hold out for better ones. However, if I could get a counter, I had a good shot at getting my price.

My offer expired in 24 hours, so I went to bed that night hoping for a response in the morning. As I lay there in silence, my mind raced. All possible outcomes, good and bad, played out like a movie in my mind. Sure enough, I received a counteroffer of $1,575,000. In 24 hours, he came down $50,000 and met me in the middle. Now it was time to negotiate. Countless hours of practicing my negotiation skills led me to this moment. The man I once was would have spat in my hand and shaken on it, but now, I knew better. The fact that he countered told me he was willing to bend. Utilizing tactics from Chris Voss's book, I vowed not to split the difference, so I drafted an email and sent it to Cameron.

Good morning,

Thank you for your counter. It's very generous, and I think it's a fair price. I apologize, but unfortunately, I can't do that. I would like to resubmit my offer of $1,500,000.
Thank you, and I hope you have a great day.

Randy J Melot
REAL ESTATE INVESTOR

Am I insane? I am one email away from going under contract and I resubmitted my previous offer instead. To say that sending that email was nerve-wracking would be an understatement. My imagination conjured the worst possible outcomes. I pictured some faceless figure reading that email and slamming his laptop, shouting, "Can you believe the nerve of this guy?" My mind raced as I waited for what felt like an eternity. I wish I could have been there to see his reaction. All I knew was that as I waited, I couldn't make a sound. I couldn't call, email, or text. I had to stay silent for this to work. It was the hardest part by far. All I could do was wait. As I refreshed my email over and over, it finally came.

I frantically opened it to see that the seller was willing to accept the purchase price but wanted to change the due diligence period from 30 days to 15 days and the closing from 45 to 30 days. I couldn't believe it. He agreed to my original offer, exactly $125,000 less than the initial price, and $75,000 less than his counteroffer. I couldn't believe what had just happened. It played out exactly how I had orchestrated it. I felt like a grandmaster forcing checkmate from twelve moves away. Of course, I wasn't really a master-level negotiator, but I had learned from the best and put their proven methods to work. With a playbook to reference and a whole lot of guts, in the end, it was simple.

Daniel taught me that when underwriting a deal, it's just as important to underwrite the person as it is to underwrite the property and the place. So I called the listing agent back to ask him a few more questions.

"Why does he want to shorten the due diligence period?

What are the tenants like?

What's the owner's screening process?

Do they pay in cash or online?

Are late payments tolerated?"

If you've ever purchased a house with an agent, you know there is a chain of communication. You ask your agent a question, they ask the seller's agent, who then asks the seller. The answer then passes through the same process until it gets back to you. Usually, you won't meet the seller until you are both sitting at the closing table, causing the information to be filtered and linear. You don't get to hear the seller's voice or see their demeanor, and you can't fully discover their core motivations. For the homebuyer, these buffers help the process move along; however, they can prevent each party from feeling like they've worked together to achieve a win. While I genuinely wanted answers to these questions, I was really trying to ask questions the agent wouldn't know so I could talk to the seller directly. A win for me is knowing that both of our goals are reached with this transaction. After my series of questions, Cameron connected me with the seller.

We started talking, and the seller had some questions for me as well. His questions were about my level of experience and which lender I was working with. At first, I found that odd. Why would he care which lender I'm using? It didn't take long to understand that he was worried I was wasting his time once he said,

"Look, you sound pretty young..."

He had been burned before and didn't want to go through two months of work just to start over, so I said,

"It sounds like you are worried that I won't be able to get funding. Is that a fair statement?"

"I just don't want to waste my time,"

he responded and my suspicions were confirmed. I

replied,

> *"How about I reach out to my lender and ask them to*
> *provide Proof of Funds (POF) and also ask if your*
> *proposed timeline is feasible? I think that will make*
> *us both feel better. Since you are shortening my due*
> *diligence period, would it be a crazy idea for you to*
> *provide me with the inspection reports from your*
> *previous buyer?*
> *That will save money and time."*

He agreed, and the conversation put us both at ease. I conveyed professionalism and capability, and he showed that he was willing to help make the deal work. We were a good fit. A few days later, we signed the contract, and we were finally underway. I knew this deal was far from a sure thing, but I was more motivated than ever before. The bulk of the work was directly ahead of me, and I was raring to go.

I took a moment to reflect on just how far I'd come. The lie many people believe is that fulfillment is found at the destination, but the truth is that joy comes from the journey. I negotiated a great deal and had a swagger in my step. My briefcase was a little lighter as I walked into work. I wasn't at the end, but I'd overcome a major milestone that excites me to this day. It's okay to enjoy the wins. In fact, it's healthy. In these moments of elation, it's important to stay focused and humble. It wasn't Icarus's waxed wings that failed but his belief that he could reach new heights without consequence. Moments in life where we are puffed up from former successes can often hinder our potential for finishing the course. Marcus Aurelius would have his servant constantly whisper in his ear, "You're just a man." The challenges that I would face in the days to come would humble me to my breaking point and undoubtedly test the measure of my resolve.

A SHIP IN HARBOR

IS SAFE, BUT THAT IS

NOT WHAT SHIPS ARE

BUILT FOR.

_____

JOHN A. SHEDD

CHAPTER EIGHT

TURNING OBSTACLES
INTO OPPORTUNITY

———————— · ——

As soon as the contract was signed, I wasted no time. With a very short due diligence period, I wanted to solidify as many variables as possible, such as insurance quotes, term sheets, inspection reports, and more. The gears were turning, and there were many moving parts. We scheduled the walkthrough for the end of the week, and I brought my dad along to view the properties with me. My dad has a background in construction and will be my property manager, so I thought it was best to leverage his expertise. When we arrived, Cameron was already there. As we waited, Cameron and I engaged in a bit of small talk, while my dad took mental notes of the property's characteristics as a blanket of humidity began to set upon us.

Once the seller arrived, we began the tour. Cameron was my age, but the seller was somewhat older and seemed to connect more with my dad. I already knew that my age concerned him, so having my dad there seemed to work in my favor. My father's bond with the seller solidified the assumption that my dad was the experienced investor and I was merely his apprentice. If it made the seller feel better, there was no sense in correcting him. I also took the opportunity to exchange contacts with Cameron, planting seeds for future relationships down the road. As we toured the building, the properties were clean, well-kept, and actively maintained, assuring me that these were quality units. Overall, the walkthrough presented no glaring red flags. The tenants we met seemed well taken care of, and any deferred maintenance, if present, would be minimal. The seller even agreed to provide me with a detailed inspection report, which would save me time and money. I left in good spirits and was ready to move forward.

Next, I needed to secure insurance. From my previous attempt at purchasing a property, I learned to make insurance my top priority. Last time, insurance was a key factor in killing the deal, so I wasted no time in making calls and getting quotes. The next obstacle was completing everything within the accelerated 15-

day due diligence period. My earnest money deposit of $30,000 is non-refundable after 15 days, so I wanted as many assurances as possible before passing the point of no return. As the deadline approached, a few things were still up in the air. I was still waiting for the trailing 12-month (T12) expense report from the seller and a few more insurance quotes. The stress was starting to compound each day. To make matters worse, my 15 days coincided with the largest annual festival in New Orleans: Mardi Gras.

Mardi Gras, which always falls on a Tuesday, essentially shuts down the entire city. Children get the entire week off from school, many businesses close for a few days, and the rest are staffed with a skeleton crew. The weeks leading up to Mardi Gras are just as eventful as the day itself, with the intensity and size of the parades growing as it gets closer to Mardi Gras Day. The city streets are filled daily with multiple parades scattered throughout the city. Even locals struggle to know exactly when and where every parade will be, causing immense traffic throughout the city due to road closures and congested areas full of pedestrians. The overall attitude and atmosphere are similar to Christmas time. Everyone is in the mood to relax and party instead of focusing on work, making conducting business during Mardi Gras nearly impossible. As my deadline loomed, I realized I just wasn't able to get everything done in time. I had come so far and now faced another ~~obstacle~~ opportunity.

I contacted Cameron to convince the seller to extend the due diligence period. I feared this might be difficult because this was the seller's win from before. He had lowered his price by $125,000 and had only asked to shorten the timeline, and now I was asking for that time back. This might seem like a bold move, but I refused to let the stress of a deadline cause me to make a poor decision. When faced with a challenge that has only one possible solution, weighing options and fearing the outcome is just more time wasted. I knew what I had to do.

"Cameron, I know the seller wanted an accelerated due diligence period, but I haven't received the T12, and I'm still waiting on insurance quotes. I've reached out to multiple agents, but it's Mardi Gras."

He responded,

"Well I think you need some more assurance before the due diligence period expires."

I said,

"How am I supposed to do that?"

He said,

"I think you should ask for an extension."

At this point, Cameron began solving my issue for me. When asking the question, "How am I supposed to do that?" you may find that people have an innate instinct to try to solve your problems. This is another technique I learned from Chris Voss. After discussing our options, the seller agreed to extend the due diligence period to 22 days. I credit this success not only to Voss's technique but also to keeping the seller in the loop. I understood from day one of signing the contract that the seller was already worried about the deal falling apart due to my youth and inexperience, so I kept them informed every step of the way. Even with the extension, I still needed to act with urgency, but after securing a favorable insurance quote, things seemed to be back on track. I provided mountains of paperwork to my lender, about ten times the amount needed for my HELOC, but I breezed through it. I was pre-approved and one step closer to closing this deal. What could go wrong?

Hello Randy,

*Programs recently changed for properties
with 9 units or more. See below:*

*Previous Interest Rate: 8.250%
Current Interest Rate: 10.74%*

I stared daggers at my computer screen. It might as well have said 80% interest because this was a deal killer. I had two days until my earnest money was no longer refundable, and this just wasn't going to work. Self-doubt flooded my mind like a waterfall because I was punching above my weight class, and now I was getting punched back. I don't have an impressive net worth or leverage with banks to secure better rates. When an investor with a multimillion dollar portfolio walks into a bank, he gets coffee and cookies in a private room, but I get shown to the back of the line. What was I thinking, trying to play with the big boys? I should throw in the towel and quit pretending before I lose $30,000.

This is when I had to decide whether I was an amateur or a professional. Would I fold under the pressure of mounting obstacles? The old me might have let this obstacle cause the deal to crumble; after all, Daniel was so proud when I backed away last time. He saw the wisdom in letting go of a large deal before. I could just do the same now, right? Does it make me wise to keep getting closer while never pulling the trigger? I can see the finish line, but do I have what it takes to finish? While an amateur focuses on the obstacle, a professional looks for an opportunity. Therefore, I reached out to an old friend.

Jeff Maher, a lifelong friend of mine, is a mortgage broker who helps homebuyers secure funding. I wanted to see if he had any contacts that might help me out of this jam. I had never thought to reach out before because he only handled residential loans, or so I thought. Unbeknownst to me, he was undergoing a transformation of his own.

About a year prior, he was working as a mortgage broker for another employer. However, during the COVID lockdowns business slowed, and his office manager was considering layoffs. Jeff, having built his team with qualified professionals he trusted, decided instead to take his team and start his own brokerage. He took the leap and was excelling, but his transformation didn't stop there. Jeff found a leading professional in the commercial loan space and built a working relationship that allowed him to learn and grow. While I was on the cusp of my first deal and Jeff was in the midst of expanding and rebranding, the stars aligned. He was able to get me pre-approved by four separate lenders in only two days with better terms than before. Even with time working against me, I was able to make a smart, calculated decision, and the deal kept moving forward. I was now past the point of no return. My due diligence period had expired; I was in uncharted waters, and now all I could do was wait.

During the time I spent waiting, I was able to reflect on this incredible journey. I had learned so much leading up to this point and even more during the purchase process. I wondered how I would have reacted two years ago if I knew I would be closing on a one-and-a-half-million-dollar deal. If someone had stopped me on the golf course in Virginia and shown me what the next two years would hold, would I have believed it? Better yet, would I have been willing to take the first step? Would I have been willing to undergo this transformation if I really understood what it would take? The crazy thing is that when you look back through the lens of having been transformed, you begin to see how trivial everything used to be. All that time wasted, and for what? Now my time is productive. I'd rather struggle through the multiple twists and turns as a real estate investor and come up short repeatedly than ever go back. I can lie my head on my pillow at night and thank God for a productive life filled with drive and tenacity. I'm no longer an outsider looking in. I am the man in the arena.

It is not the critic who counts; not the man who points out how the strong man stumbles, or where the doer of deeds could have done them better. The credit belongs to the man who is actually in the arena, whose face is marred by dust and sweat and blood; who strives valiantly; who errs, who comes short again and again, because there is no effort without error and shortcoming; but who does actually strive to do the deeds; who knows great enthusiasms, the great devotions; who spends himself in a worthy cause; who at the best knows in the end the triumph of high achievement, and who at the worst, if he fails, at least fails while daring greatly, so that his place shall never be with those cold and timid souls who neither know victory nor defeat.

-Theodore Roosevelt

It's Tuesday, April 16, 2024. I've carefully decided what to wear, and my clothes are laid out for the morning. My briefcase is packed, and I have everything I need. The big day is finally here. We are mere hours away from one of the greatest moments in my life. Tomorrow, my son, Samuel, will be born. That's right. For the last nine months, in the midst of changing careers and working harder than ever, my wife has stood by my side with a baby on the way. Everything has happened in God's timing. After a year of praying and a word from God, Lisa was pregnant in His timing. After a year of undergoing one transformation after another, talking to countless sellers, negotiating deals, making offers, and signing contracts, the timing of this deal has come according to God's design. The birth of my first deal is in the same season as the birth of my son. Purchasing this property will be a by-product of a lifestyle I've adopted. My goal was always to build something sustainable and do it all for the glory of God. Not just sustainable in my lifetime, but something my children will inherit and grow. My son will always know that when he came into this world, his dad was working toward his future. My number one priority in life is to do God's will and to do right by my family.

As my children grow up, they will see their dad always striving to be a better version of himself as I teach them to do the same. They will see that their parents' motivations are aligned with God's will. They will witness as I achieve success only to pass it on and accumulate wealth only to generously give it away. As I lead my family, they will see the fruits of the Spirit developed in my life to become successful according to God's call on my life. Tomorrow, gratitude will fill my heart and lead me to the next deal. Gratitude that God has allowed me to travel this path and has equipped me to take on greater responsibility. My legacy won't be a billion-dollar portfolio or a staggering net worth, but one of gratitude and love for God. That is what I will pass on to my children, every day, in everything I do.

I am grateful for the lessons I've learned this past year and the accomplishments that gave me confidence. I'm grateful for the relationships that have been forged and strengthened. I'm thankful that God has given me a mentor to guide me and that my own transformation has enhanced the lives of others. I'm thankful that this book found its way into your hands to make an impact on your life. Your transformation will enhance even more lives, and the exponential impact will grow beyond my reach. Most of all, I am so thankful to finally close my very first deal. Wait, did I close the deal, right?

YET WHO KNOWS
WHETHER YOU HAVE COME
TO THE KINGDOM FOR
SUCH A TIME AS THIS?

———————————————

ESTHER 4:14 NKJV

CHAPTER NINE

FOR SUCH A TIME AS THIS

————————— · —

Sitting in the hospital room, exhausted beyond belief, my newborn was in the NICU. He was born at 7:00 a.m. and spent most of the day with us until about 4:00 p.m. that evening. My daughter and parents were with us, rejoicing in his arrival only to have the nurses whisk him away for specialized treatment. Samuel needed some respiratory assistance, so they moved him to a separate floor. The emotions were every variation of high and low; as you can imagine, real estate was the last thing on my mind.

Jeff was doing his best not to bother me unless absolutely necessary, but on his end, my loan was falling apart. I needed to extend the closing date multiple times, and the seller's patience was wearing thin. While the clock ticked faster and faster, the lender was delaying the entire process. I had insurance, title, surveys, appraisals, and conditions met, but the lender refused to move with urgency. In between assisting my wife with feedings and visiting my son in the NICU, I was answering emails and taking phone calls, but the reality was that this deal was slipping through my hands. If that wasn't enough, other problems began to arise. One of the bank's conditions, cleared two months prior, was now being flagged. Then, suddenly, the lender withdrew the loan. By the time I found out, Jeff was already working with another bank. The deal was on life support as we proceeded to extend the contract yet again. In the days that followed, a vicious pattern started to emerge. What seemed like an endless loop of denial repeated over and over:

Step One: Find a bank willing to work with us

Step Two: Provide information needed to underwrite the loan

Step Three: Notify the seller and extend the contract

Step Four: Discuss my experience and financial situation with a bank representative

Step Five: Advance to underwriting and await final approval

Step Six: Get Denied

We went through this process six times over the course of 45 days, and it always ended the same. Most of the banks disliked my lack of experience or thought I didn't have enough liquidity. Some disapproved of me using an investor. One bank actually preferred that I have a traditional mortgage instead of a HELOC. The bottom line was that financial institutions are in the business of mitigating risk, and for one reason or another, I was deemed too risky.

After allowing this process to drag on for far too long, the seller wanted to charge me for any further extensions. What do I do now? I had done everything I knew, but it just wasn't in the cards. There is a fine line between determination and insanity, but never before had the lines blurred as much as they did at this moment. Do I pay the seller to extend the contract and risk being denied six more times? Do I walk away after all I have invested? This is why so many people lose money at casinos. The gambler is in too deep and isn't strong enough to walk away. Instead of losing $100, he continues to gamble until he loses thousands, and it's all gone. I may be in deep, but I refuse to become "pot committed." I would rather lose some money and walk away than lose it all. After exhausting every possible outcome, time was up. I made the hardest and most painful call yet. I decided not to pay to extend the contract, so it defaulted. I made a tough decision in a no-win situation; so, how much did I lose? I lost my earnest money deposit, plus the amount I spent on appraisals and surveys. Altogether, I lost $42,000 in the span of 3½ months.

In the aftermath, it was time for some inward reflection. I became brutally honest with myself as I wondered if I was really cut out for this line of work. Do I truly possess the risk tolerance required to fight my way to success? My thoughts were loud and relentless, with some saying I messed up and others suggesting I made the right choice. Additionally, there were the constant replays in my head of lenders saying, "Denied!" louder each time. Getting back up was a challenge, but I decided to focus on what really mattered.

My son made a quick recovery, and we left the hospital together as a family. We were home, adjusting to a new way of life. My daughter, Lila, was now a big sister, and my wife and I were overjoyed to be holding our baby boy. Nothing puts things in perspective quite like staring into the eyes of your newborn and spending time with your family. The people I care about and love most in this world are depending on me. I can't say exactly how I might have reacted in different circumstances, but at this moment, though I may have lost money, I knew I was not a failure. Even more so, I knew that God had not failed me. Regardless, the decisions I make now will shape the future for my family; the rest are just obstacles in my past. What lessons will I have to teach my children? Will I be able to one day look them in the eye and teach them the importance of perseverance in the face of adversity? I soon realized I feared regret much more than failure. As costly as this setback was, it will not be the end of my story.

This is not the first time I've had a deal fall through. If you recall, I was under contract back in November of 2023, and when that deal fell through, I was able to walk away unscathed. This time, it was different—a $42,000 kind of difference. Somehow, I was in a better mental state this time around. Even though I had to find another deal, I wasn't really starting back at square one. Last time, I was so focused on the deal at hand that I ignored all other possibilities. After walking away from this experience, I learned that a sustainable business model needs to keep moving forward. Even when in the midst of a deal, I should be looking at other opportunities. I needed to keep my deal channels alive because they would be the lifeline to my business, so I continued to leverage previously formed relationships while considering other deals.

A few weeks passed as I searched for more deals, and I noticed that the two properties I had failed to close on were back on the market. Originally listed as a portfolio sale, they were now separate listings. I also observed that the price had increased by a quarter of a million dollars, totaling $1.75 million. To briefly recap the properties, the Uptown property had 10 units, and the Bywater property had 8 units. The Uptown property was in a better location, better condition, and housed a more loyal clientele. In February, I had asked Cameron if the seller was interested in selling only the Uptown property, but the answer was no. It confused me to see it back on the market in this manner. It also made me wonder if the banks would have approved the deal if I had only wanted one property. I was overwhelmed with thoughts that were quite paralyzing. It pained me slightly to see what was almost mine back on the market. Everyone says not to be emotional in business, but I've come to realize that's virtually impossible. A better approach is not to let your emotions drive your decisions, so I put my emotions aside and continued working. I got back to grinding and kept my mind off the deal, but then the phone rang.

"You're not going to believe this. We applied with another bank, and you've been approved. They just need the Supervisor to sign off on it." -Jeff

My thoughts were explosive as my heart pounded. How? Why? Why now when it's too late? I didn't even know Jeff was still trying to get my deal approved. I had moved on, the properties were back on the market, and I had accepted the loss of my earnest money. I had, to the best of my ability, come to terms with the reality that this deal was dead. We had done the autopsy, held the funeral, and eaten the donuts. Now, after burying this deal, I get approved? How could this be? What will the seller think? I have frustrated him even more than the banks did to me. As clarity and adrenaline fused in my mind, I called Cameron and began,

"You're not gonna believe this...."

Cameron exclaimed,

"You got approved!"

He already knew. I think he could sense it in my voice. From what I could tell, he was happy to hear the news. While they had received a few offers and were in the middle of negotiating a counter, the properties were still not under contract. I was still reeling from the news, but there was one issue: I could not put down another deposit. Quite frankly, I was out of money.

Whether I was willing to or not didn't matter; I simply didn't have the capital for another deposit. If I were to go back under contract, I was only willing to re-enter the agreement with the seller under the previous terms. Of course, he could refuse, and I would still be out $42,000, but I was determined to make a wise choice, not an emotional one. I told Cameron and sent him the commitment letter from the bank. In the loan process, a commitment letter is the most concrete assurance a person can have besides the actual money itself.

At this point, I felt that Cameron was rooting for me, and I even thought the seller was rooting for me. I had a good chance of reviving this deal, but in any real estate transaction, there are two currencies: time and money. When negotiating, you leverage one of the two. At the beginning of this deal, I had negotiated a good price, but as the process moved forward, it took more time than expected. It was a tough spot to be in, but I had to try, so it was time to talk to the seller. I already knew what his response would be, and I am sure you do too. In short, he wanted more money.

The seller was willing to proceed, but he would honor only $10,000 of the original $30,000 deposit. This was not a bad offer and could even be considered fair, but I couldn't come up with another $20,000. I told

Cameron that the entire $30,000 would have to apply. A day later, the seller offered another $5,000, and then another $5,000 the day after that. He was now willing to honor $20,000, and I would have to pay $10,000. I still couldn't do it. Make no mistake, while this was some of the boldest negotiations I had performed, it wasn't out of an evil intent to squeeze or take advantage of him. It was just the facts. He could have countered one dollar at a time, and the answer would have been the same. The question you should be asking is why the seller continued to entertain these negotiations if I was unwilling to budge. The truth is that I had something no one else had: assurance that I could purchase the properties faster than any other buyer. He could move on and find other buyers, but that would take much longer than making a deal with me. If my deal was good enough two weeks ago, then it would have to be good enough today. After I refused a third time, the seller asked if he could call me directly.

Before our conversation, I really wanted to see things from his perspective. Knowing he was a married man discussing this deal with his wife, I decided to get my wife's perspective as well. I asked her if she thought I should get my entire $30,000 deposit credited to the sale. She emphatically replied that I should. A good wife will fight for you, stand by you, and often see things from your perspective. I then asked her to imagine we were selling the properties.

> *"Pretend that we entered into this deal in February, and it's now June. The buyers have extended the contract countless times. After months of waiting, to no fault of our own, the buyer couldn't get approved. We cashed a $30,000 check for time wasted and went our separate ways. Then, weeks later, that same buyer calls and wants back in the deal, and he wants the $30,000 that's rightfully ours to be redeemed. The buyer wants to give us the exact amount we asked for, but nearly six months later. We have countered time and time again, but he is unwilling to budge."*

Her countenance changed as she replied, "

> *I see your point."*

I asked her,

> *"How do I get him to agree?"*

She replied,

> *"You have to appeal to his emotions."*

He was afraid that I wouldn't be able to close, so I had to alleviate that fear. When we finally spoke, he started by offering another concession, but it was moot at this point. I explained that the margins were tight due to the price of insurance, that I had a duty to my investor, and that the money I would be paying him would have to come out of my operating reserves. I apologized for the inconvenience of the obstacles we had encountered and simply explained that we would have to pick up where we left off. I also told him that I understood that this had taken longer than expected, and unless he had a cash offer, I would be his quickest way out of this deal. I tried to put us on the same team by explaining that I was frustrated too. While this was a negotiation tactic, it was undoubtedly true. The banks kept telling me everything looked good and then, at the last minute, pulled the rug out from under me. He asked,

"How can I know that this time you will be able to close?"

That was the core of his fears. I took a deep breath, remembered my wife's advice, and appealed to his emotions. I said,

"I understand why you feel that way, and if I were in

your shoes, I would be asking the very same thing.
This time the bank has actually given me a letter of
commitment and my mortgage broker would be
willing to talk to you and verify that."

He replied,

"The mortgage broker can say that all day
long, but it's really up to the bank."

"You're right. How about I reach out to the loan officer
who issued the letter and ask her to give you a call?"

One of my favorite stories in the Bible is the story of Joseph. As a young man, Joseph had a promise from God that he would be a great leader, only to be betrayed, sold into slavery, falsely convicted, and forgotten in prison. After years of what looked like hopelessness, his dream suffered a long, agonizing death. Yet, God remembered Joseph and resurrected his dream. God poured out His favor on Joseph, and he was promoted to a high position in the land, second in command to Pharaoh. He was tasked with storing food for the coming famine and he was able to provide food to all of Egypt as well as nearby lands. His own brothers even traveled to Egypt during the famine to purchase food. They were grateful that Joseph was there to supply the needs of the kingdom. He was only able to fulfill his potential in God's timing. Every step along the way, from the pit to the prison, then to the palace, was essential in fulfilling Joseph's destiny.

As I felt this deal breathing new life, I remembered the story of Joseph. I remembered that, like Joseph, God made me a promise too. I did everything I could, and only when there was nothing left for me to do did God resurrect my deal.

"...and having done all, to stand. Stand...." - Ephesians 6:13-14

The phone call with the loan officer must have gone well because the seller called me back the next day and offered me a choice. First, he said he would honor my deposit in full. If I wanted to buy both properties, he would increase the price by $50,000 or I could purchase the uptown property only for the previously agreed-upon price of $833,000. From the beginning, I only wanted the uptown property. Now, months later, he is placing it on a platter right in front of me. I can make a larger down payment, which will result in higher cash flow and $400,000 in equity at the closing. This deal is as solid as they come. Just as Joseph had to endure the death of his dream to realize God's promise, I had to endure every heart-wrenching denial to end up with the property I wanted all along—and more importantly, the one God had for me.

At last, the long-awaited day has arrived. July 23, 2024, is closing day. I've finally reached the end of what has been by far the most challenging career move of my life. The man I once was, lying on the floor in Virginia, is no more. As I button my coat and grab my briefcase, the man in the mirror has evolved. The decision to take the leap, the disappointments and heartaches, the little wins, the lessons learned, and transformation after transformation have led me to this very moment. I've consistently stated that it's about the journey, but I am glad to have reached the end. The heights God has brought me far outway the struggles that got me here. From my first phone call with Cameron to closing day is exactly 180 days. In the very long span of six months, much longer than I had hoped, I increased my unit count tenfold. I went from "getting into real estate" to "I'm a real estate investor" as my life took a 180-degree turn toward my future. I stand on the peak of the highest mountain thus far. With each step, I expanded my network, learned from experience, and elevated my status. I also welcomed my son into the world, made my mentors proud, and made my wife even prouder. As I stand on the peak and look into the horizon, I await the next adventure.

This deal is not the end of my story; it's my launching pad. My transformation is not complete; I've just been primed to transform again. Every finish line is the beginning of the next journey. I am not sure what the future holds, but if the last two years of my life were this transformative, imagine what your life can be. I had no clue that I would be closing a deal and writing a book about it. Now, I realize this book is far greater than my first deal. This book is here to inspire you to start your journey and take that first step. Even while writing this, I am aware that the real work takes place after I write the last sentence. I'll have to reach out to people who have published books of their own for advice, as I partner with other professionals and overcome even more obstacles. By the time this book launches, I'll be a different version of myself than the one writing now. By the time we hear incredible stories of people transforming, excelling, and stepping into their destiny, the work will already be done. You are reading about when I closed my first deal in 2024. It may be 5, 10, 20 years, or more since that took place. All the incredible things that await me in my future may already be in the past. Everything I had to do to get here, I've done a long time ago. When can I say the same about you?

Success is not just for the privileged. Happiness

does not come by chance. Empires are not forged by the timid. Risk is not reserved for the experienced. Everyone's journey is different, but what we all share is the beginning. The time to change your circumstances is now. Your transformation begins today. Will it be hard? Yes. Will you breeze through? Definitely not. There's plenty to fear, but for the determined, there's nothing to fear. As you look up at the mountain from the bottom, the top is barely visible. For every one of you, there are a thousand reasons to quit, but I implore you to forget your circumstances and ignore your doubts. Face your fears and start climbing because you were made for such a time as this.

IF YOU WANT SOMETHING
YOU HAVE NEVER HAD,
YOU MUST BE WILLING TO
DO SOMETHING YOU HAVE
NEVER DONE.

———————————

THOMAS JEFFERSON

CHAPTER TEN

FIVE STEPS TO
TRANSFORMATION

———————— .

Since I started my business, my goal has been to be a better real estate investor today than I was yesterday. I have shared a glimpse of the circumstances and obstacles I have encountered along the way. My journey will not look like yours, but whatever your destination may be, there is one thing that we share: the need to change. "People don't change," or so they say. Phrases like that are indicative of a society seeking comfort over progress. If we believe we "are who we are" with no hope of improvement, then we are victims of our circumstances. To break from the script and take control of our future, we need to undergo a transformation. My transformation occurred in five identifiable phases:

AWAKENING | DECISION | KNOWLEDGE
IMPLEMENTATION | GROWTH

AWAKENING

The awakening is the moment in time that changes your trajectory forever. It is the sudden realization that things can be different. My awakening occurred when I learned about HELOCs and the velocity banking strategy. When your awakening takes place and a new path emerges, it is up to you to recognize it. If you sense an awakening in your spirit and a fire in your belly, perhaps it is time to feed the flame. I believe that God gives us vision, but we have to seek Him to find it. Without vision, there is no path and, therefore, no destination. Embrace your vision, whether it is financial freedom, new frontiers, or personal change. This can be your moment, your epiphany, and your chance to cut ties with the marionette that has strung you along like a puppet. Take the reins, chart a new course, think outside the box, and take a chance. Discover your passion and be passionate about it. Your transformation is one step away.

DECISION

If you decide to be one of the few who dares to venture into unfamiliar territory, do so with your eyes open and be fully aware of the cost. Decide who you want to become, then break down your vision into everyday action items. Don't just cut out bad habits; replace them with new ones. Replace comfort with motivation. Replace excuses with solutions. Remember, the old you cannot achieve new results, so create a new version of yourself and embrace this new identity.

KNOWLEDGE

It will become clear what knowledge you lack, so seek the knowledge that will keep you moving forward. It takes humility to acknowledge that you need a mentor, but true confidence is the ability to be transparent and say, "I don't know." Joining AREA was my first step to gaining the knowledge necessary to achieve my goals. I set aside my autonomous tendencies in favor of learning from experts. Whichever path you have chosen, there is someone who has already walked it and marked each obstacle. Smart people learn from their mistakes, but wise people learn from the mistakes of others. Access to knowledge has never been more attainable, so the only excuse for why you aren't where you want to be is you. Read books, listen to podcasts, and learn from mentors. Each time you reach a new level of competence in your field, it provides the opportunity to learn even more and increase your expertise. Just like the crawl, walk, run analogy, with each thing you learn, you unlock the ability to learn even more and keep moving forward.

IMPLEMENTATION

"Do you give the horse its strength or clothe its neck with a flowing mane? Do you make it leap like a locust, striking terror with its proud snorting? It paws fiercely, rejoicing in its strength, and charges into the fray. It laughs at fear, afraid of nothing; it does not shy away from the sword. The quiver rattles against its side, along with the flashing spear and lance. In frenzied excitement it eats up the ground; it cannot stand still when the trumpet sounds. At the blast of the trumpet it snorts, 'Aha!' It catches the scent of battle from afar, the shout of commanders and the battle cry."

- Job 39:19-25

Now is your time. Take action by doing. Go to conferences, set up meetings, get productive, make calls, make deals, take advice, learn from failure, and never give up. Surround yourself with people who believe in your vision and believe in you. When I gave up on my HELOC, it was my wife who pushed me to keep going. Who will take this ride with you? Partner with people who are going through transformations of their own. Have faith that God will help you on your journey, and that you are worthy of success. Nothing about changing your circumstances will be easy, but that is what sets you apart.

GROWTH

Growth is the natural by-product of everything stated above. As you begin to grow, measure your growth consistently. I chose to measure growth by journaling. Just as a profit and loss statement measures the growth of a company, a journal measures the growth of an individual. In addition to recapping the day's events, I always list three wins from the day and three goals for the next day. The wins provide motivation to continue the following day, while the goals give you direction first thing in the morning. This tactic was coined by Dr. Benjamin Hardy in his book *The Gap and the Gain*. As Dr. Hardy explains, if you focus only on the end result, you may feel unaccomplished and inadequate. However, if you measure your growth as your transformation takes place, it builds your confidence and expands your horizon. This will change your perspective and empower you to strive for the next mountaintop. Once I started doing this, I was able to avoid the trap of staying busy while accomplishing nothing. The greatest failure in life is being productive without being effective.

CONCLUSION

If you have read this far, hopefully, you have felt a stirring within yourself. Make this your awakening. Start your journal and mark today as the day you decided to break free. It is my sincere hope that you will strive for something greater than yourself. Begin your personal transformation. Whatever God has in store for you is within your reach. You need only to take that step.

TODAY IS THE DAY!

ACCELERATED REAL ESTATE ACADEMY

At Accelerated Real Estate Academy, the mission is to equip and empower individuals not only to complete real estate deals but to become real estate entrepreneurs who achieve financial freedom. This freedom enables them to spend more time doing what they love, rather than being confined to a traditional 9-to-5 job.

Daniel and Sam Kwak accomplish this by helping new and beginning investors break through obstacles and learn to navigate the world of real estate like never before. I, Randy Millet, am a prime example of their impact. Through their guidance, I have transformed into the real estate investor you have just read about. The journey was challenging, but it was undoubtedly worth it.

I challenge you to take the first step today. Scan the QR code below to begin your journey as a real estate investor. I look forward to seeing you at the next Mastermind.

REFERENCES

Asch Conformity Experiment Asch, S. E. (1956).
Studies of Independence and Conformity: I.
A Minority of One Against a Unanimous Majority.
Psychological Monographs: General and Applied,
70(9), 1–70.

Hill, N. (2023). Think and Grow Rich: Complete and
Original Signature Edition. Maple Spring
Publishing.

King, S. (1995). The Shawshank Redemption. Time
Warner Paperbacks.

Kiyosaki, R. T., & Lechter, S. L. (2002). Rich Dad, Poor
Dad: What the Rich Teach Their Kids About Money.
Sphere.

Kwak, D., Kwak, S., & McPherson, L. (2020). 0 to 75
Units in Just 1 year: Introducing the FORCE
Strategy to Acquiring Rental Properties. Indy Pub.

Sullivan, D., & Hardy, B. (2021). The Gap and the Gain:
The High Achievers' Guide to Happiness, Confidence,
and Success. Hay House.

Thomas Nelson Publishers. (2003). King James Version Bible.
World Bible.

Voss, C., & Raz, T. (2019). Never Split the Difference: Negotiating
As If Your Life Depended on It. Cornerstone Digital.

GLOSSARY

Accelerated Banking Consulting Program (ABC)

ABC is a program led by Sam Kwak that offers members expert insights and strategies for mastering banking and financial management.

Accelerated Real Estate Academy (AREA)

AREA, founded by Daniel Kwak, is a program that offers expert mentorship and guidance tailored specifically for real estate investors.

Acquisition Process

The steps and procedures involved in acquiring a property or business. It includes identifying a target, performing due diligence, negotiating terms, and finalizing the purchase.

BAMFAM

"Book A Meeting From A Meeting." This is a sales strategy to ensure that before ending a meeting, you schedule the next one, keeping the momentum going.

Capitalization Rates (CAP Rates)

A real estate metric used to evaluate the return on

investment of a property. It's calculated by dividing the property's net operating income (NOI) by its current market value.

Debt-to-Income Ratio (DTI)

A financial metric that compares an individual's total monthly debt payments to their gross monthly income. Lenders use this ratio to assess a borrower's ability to manage monthly payments and repay debts. A lower DTI indicates a more manageable debt level relative to income, making it easier to qualify for loans.

Due Diligence Period

The time frame in which a buyer can investigate a property or business before finalizing the purchase. This involves reviewing financials, legal documents, and conducting inspections to ensure there are no hidden issues.

Earnest Money Deposit

A deposit made by a buyer to show their serious intent to purchase a property. It is typically held in escrow and applied toward the purchase price if the sale goes through.

Home Equity Line of Credit (HELOC)

A revolving line of credit that allows homeowners to borrow against the equity in their home. It functions similarly to a credit card, where you can borrow, repay, and borrow again up to a certain limit.

Letter of Intent (LOI)

A non-binding document outlining the basic terms and conditions of a potential deal, often used in the early stages of negotiations for real estate or business acquisitions.

Limited Partner

An investor who contributes capital but does not participate in day-to-day management. They have limited liability, meaning their losses are limited to the amount they invested.

Loan-to-Value (LTV)

A ratio that compares the amount of a loan to the value of the asset purchased. It's used by lenders to assess the risk of lending, with a lower LTV indicating less risk.

Multiple Listing Service (MLS)

A database used by real estate brokers to list properties for sale. It's a centralized system that allows agents to share information about properties with other agents and potential buyers.

Net Operating Income (NOI)

A measure of a property's profitability. It's calculated by subtracting operating expenses from gross income, excluding taxes, interest, and capital expenditures.

Proof of Funds (POF)

> A document or statement that shows a buyer has the
> financial resources to complete a transaction. It's often
> required in real estate deals to prove that the buyer can
> cover the purchase price or down payment.

Tactical Empathy

> A negotiating technique that involves understanding
> and acknowledging the emotions and perspectives of
> the other party to build trust and find common ground.

Trailing Twelve Months (T12)

> A financial term that refers to the last twelve consecutive
> months of a company's or property's performance. It's
> used to analyze recent performance, often in terms of
> revenue, expenses, or cash flow.

Wholesaling

> A real estate investment strategy where an investor
> contracts a property with a seller and then finds a buyer
> to purchase it at a higher price, making a profit from the
> difference. The wholesaler typically never actually buys
> the property but acts as a middleman.